The Edges of Education

Complicated Conversation

A Book Series of Curriculum Studies

William F. Pinar.
Series Editor

Volume 64

Peter Roberts

THE EDGES OF EDUCATION

Limits and Possibilities

PETER LANG

New York · Berlin · Bruxelles · Chennai · Lausanne · Oxford

Library of Congress Cataloging-in-Publication Data

Names: Roberts, Peter, 1963- author.
Title: The edges of education : limits and possibilities / Peter Roberts.
Description: New York : Peter Lang, [2025] | Series: Complicated conversation, 1534-2816; vol. 64 | Includes bibliographical references and index.
Identifiers: LCCN 2025000654 (print) | LCCN 2025000655 (ebook) | ISBN 9783034351768 (paperback) | ISBN 9783034351751 (hardback) | ISBN 9783034354189 (pdf) | ISBN 9783034354196 (epub)
Subjects: LCSH: Education–Philosophy. | Learning–Philosophy.
Classification: LCC LB14.7 .R6224 2025 (print) | LCC LB14.7 (ebook) | DDC 370.1–dc23/eng/20250205
LC record available at https://lccn.loc.gov/2025000654
LC ebook record available at https://lccn.loc.gov/2025000655

Bibliographic information published by the Deutsche Nationalbibliothek. The German National Library lists this publication in the German National Bibliography; detailed bibliographic data is available on the Internet at http://dnb.d-nb.de.

Cover image: © Peter Roberts
Cover design by Peter Lang Group AG

ISSN 1534-2816
ISBN 978-3-0343-5176-8 (PB) (print)
ISBN 978-3-0343-5175-1 (HB) (print)
ISBN 978-3-0343-5418-9 (ePDF)
ISBN 978-3-0343-5418-9 (ePub)
DOI 10.3726/b22717

© 2025 Peter Lang Group AG, Lausanne
Published by Peter Lang Publishing Inc., New York, USA
info@peterlang.com – www.peterlang.com

All rights reserved.
All parts of this publication are protected by copyright.
Any utilization outside the strict limits of the copyright law, without the permission of the publisher, is forbidden and liable to prosecution.
This applies in particular to reproductions, translations, microfilming, and storage and processing in electronic retrieval systems.

This publication has been peer reviewed.

CONTENTS

Introduction:	The Edges of Education: Limits and Possibilities	1
Chapter 1.	Nature, Reason and Education: Learning with Leopardi	15
Chapter 2.	'The Clear Eye of the World': Schopenhauer on Pure Contemplation	39
Chapter 3.	Education and the Ethics of Attention: The Work of Simone Weil	65
Chapter 4.	The Stranger as Teacher: Maxine Greene, Madness and the Mystery of Education	85
Chapter 5.	Education, Death and Immortality: From Unamuno to Beauvoir and Beyond	107
	Credits	131
	Index	133

INTRODUCTION

THE EDGES OF EDUCATION: LIMITS AND POSSIBILITIES

We often hold high hopes for education. In some respects, these expectations are not unreasonable. Education can provide opportunities to gain qualifications that will lead to a wider range of employment options, higher incomes and improvements in standards of living. In learning to read and write, we open up new possibilities for communication and creativity. We are granted access to domains of knowledge that might otherwise be closed to us. Education can enable more informed participation in civic life and enhance our understanding of other cultures and worldviews. It can bring us into contact with others who share a similar passion for study and introduce us to teachers who can serve as lifelong role models. The research undertaken at higher levels in the education system can, when applied in practical and professional contexts, help us to build safer bridges, design healthier homes and probe the outer limits of space. It can lead to life-saving discoveries in medicine and pivotal advances in the cultivation of the food we need to survive. Education can be entertaining, engaging and enjoyable. Given the myriad benefits associated with education, it is not difficult to see why governments around the world invest billions of dollars in it every year, supporting kindergartens, schools, universities and other institutions.

There is, however, a more unsettling side to education that is seldom discussed. A commitment to education involves more than the acquisition of skills or facts; it implies a process of coming to know ourselves and the world. The prospect of expanding our awareness in this way will often be welcomed. But, as the thinkers examined in this book show, deepening our understanding of the realities of human existence can also be a distressing experience. Our capacity for reflective thought has been vital in our evolution and development as a species, but it can also become a curse. At an individual level, a critical consciousness, once formed, will not let us go; it cannot simply be switched on or off as we choose. We must, instead, learn to live with the consequences of a shift in our orientation toward the world – with the 'disease' that is consciousness (Unamuno, 1972) – and this can be painful and uncomfortable. Education can involve a harrowing process of what Weil (1997) refers to as 'decreation', where we must stare into a void of despair, sometimes with no obvious consolation or way out. Education, conceived in this manner, makes life harder, not easier. It may allow us to appreciate art and nature in new ways, but it can also lead to profound unhappiness (Leopardi, 2014). Having started down an educational path, our relationships and our sense of what we stand for, and why, can begin to change. Friendships can be tested, and allegiances may be questioned. What was unambiguous or straightforward for us in the past may now seem frustratingly complicated. Seeking further knowledge will sometimes take us no closer to 'solving' the problems we face; indeed, it can add to our difficulties, for the desire to know, like many other desires, can never be fully satisfied (Schopenhauer, 1966a, 1966b). In short, while we may continue to enjoy many of the advantages conferred by education, we must also be prepared for new challenges, not just for the duration of a given programme of study but for the rest of our lives.

    This does not mean we should abandon our pedagogical efforts. Teaching and learning remain important not just in spite of these unsettling aspects of educational experience but *because* of them. Education is *meant* to make us restless, meant to shake us up and prod us to look again at what we thought we knew. Teaching can, and arguably should, be a 'subversive' activity (Postman & Weingartner, 1971). Teachers can raise questions themselves and foster the same inquisitive and investigative spirit in others. Our ability to ask questions is one of the distinguishing features of being human. Questions may be prompted by idle curiosity or casual observation, but they may also be highlighted for us by others, either directly (e.g. through face-to-face interaction in a classroom) or indirectly (e.g. via a book). Questions can lead to ground-breaking findings in science and to great works of art. They can serve as a source of fascination and motivation, driving us to inquire further. But they can also trouble us, ethically and existentially, leaving us feeling uneasy, uncertain and concerned.[1] This discomfort is, however, an essential element of any well-rounded approach to education, and such states of mind are perhaps more needed today than ever before. Admitting to doubts, retaining an openness to different ways of addressing human problems and being prepared to change are attributes often in short supply. These qualities should be valued rather than denigrated or despised.

We live in an age of exaggerated certainties. Capitalism appears to have trumped all other modes of social and economic organisation and is frequently touted as the only possible way forward for 'developed' and 'developing' countries alike.[2] Fascism, with its emphasis on entrenched intolerance and hatred, has never entirely disappeared and continues to morph into new forms. Religious extremism, with believers who seem unable to comprehend or respect other faiths and cultural traditions, remains an ever-present threat. In education too, we have witnessed the emergence of new discourses of certainty. Science is frequently seen as the only legitimate arbiter on matters of educational debate. We are led to believe that if we can find out enough about the human brain, we will unlock the mysteries of education and discover the best approaches to teaching and learning. Funding agencies expect new developments in education to be 'evidence-based', as if questions relating to what counts as evidence, for whom, in what ways and under what circumstances require no debate. Trends come and go, but at any given time, those responsible for making decisions about the direction of education – in the teaching of reading, in curriculum content or in classroom organisation, for example – often act as if there can be little doubt about what is needed.[3] Certainty is treated as a sign of strength. This book offers an alternative perspective: one based on an ethical and aesthetic account of education, where critical engagement with the work of a range of nineteenth- and twentieth-century philosophers, poets, novelists and educationists yields a renewed appreciation of the importance of *un*certainty in human life.

---

1   As Simone de Beauvoir (1948) points out, while tyrants can rest on the certainty of their aims, others have to endure the 'painfulness of an indefinite questioning' (p. 133).
2   It is recognised that the terms 'developed' and 'developing' are problematic. They are employed here as this is the language frequently used by politicians and policy organisations in reinforcing, explicitly or implicitly, the need for continuing capitalist expansion and growth. Other terms such as 'First World' and 'Third World' have been adopted in the past as an alternative way of grouping countries. Among academics, it is more common today to distinguish between the global 'North' and the global 'South'.
3   A recent example from the New Zealand context is the complete shift, with a change in government, to 'structured literacy' as the mandated approach to reading instruction in schools.

An 'ethics of ambiguity', as Simone de Beauvoir (1948) calls it, is a powerful corrective to the excessive certainties of our current age precisely because it proceeds from a starting point of fragility, of contingency in human decisions and actions. *The Edges of Education: Limits and Possibilities* maintains that in seeking to understand the meaning, purpose and value of education, our starting point should not be performance, productivity or prosperity but rather the existing human individual (Kierkegaard, 2009). A focus on the question of existence helps us to see that attempts to turn education into a science, with readily identifiable, clear-cut objectives and measurable outcomes, are misplaced. This book suggests that much of what matters most in education resists the logic of quantification, classification and categorisation. Education can be unpredictable and unruly. It can be as much about the unknown as it is about the known. It can deepen our appreciation for mystery and wonder. Acknowledging the importance of the aesthetic and ethical dimensions of education allows us to explore realms of human experience that may hitherto have been hidden from us.[4] The obsession with measuring almost every aspect of human life – with reducing so much of what we do to a numbers game – creates its own blindness, and education has a pivotal role to play in restoring the sight that has been lost in this madness. Education, this book contends, should enable us to inhabit spaces – intellectual, emotional and spiritual – that cannot be adequately understood or explained via the language of rankings and ratings, indices and indicators, league tables and lists. The spaces signalled here constitute the 'edges' of education, rarely recognised or acknowledged in official policy documents and school curriculum statements, but rich with potential for revealing more of the subtleties, the complexities – the fullness – of human life. The spaces we occupy in seeking an education of this kind will often be surprising, at times joyful, but also potentially painful and upsetting. These are conceptual and lived modes of existence that often blur the boundaries between the possible and the impossible, setting limits while also opening up unexpected opportunities for teaching and learning. They are there for us all to experience, if only we can open our eyes to see them and muster the courage to investigate them.

The Edges of Education has been conceived, from the beginning, as a companion volume to an earlier sole-authored work, *Happiness, Hope, and Despair: Rethinking the Role of Education* (Roberts, 2016). That book was itself the culmination of a long process of reflection, reading and writing. It was an

---

4   On the importance of aesthetic education, see D'Olimpio (2024).

attempt to probe a little further in terrain that remained, at that stage, relatively unexplored by educationists.[5] There had been no shortage of scholarship on happiness, but little had been said about the educational significance of despair.[6] *The Edges of Education* builds upon and extends key ideas developed in *Happiness, Hope, and Despair*. It introduces new literary figures, philosophers and educationists – Leopardi, Schopenhauer, Beauvoir, Cervantes and Greene, among others – and it approaches those who were considered in the earlier volume (Unamuno and Weil in particular) in new ways. The portrait of the human condition painted by some of these writers is, on the surface, rather grim. Leopardi, Schopenhauer and Unamuno can be seen as representatives of what Joshua Dienstag (2006) refers to as the pessimistic tradition. In their philosophical musings, there is an open acknowledgement of the unhappiness and despair that characterises many lives. Education, they recognise, can sharpen and intensify our sense that all is not well. Leopardi, Schopenhauer and Unamuno show that in seeking to know, in a rational and critical fashion, we can find ourselves perpetually dissatisfied. We cannot overcome our difficulties through further study and learning. Instead, we keep struggling and suffering, the inner turmoil we experience sometimes being matched – as was the case for Leopardi – with extreme physical discomfort. Yet, for these thinkers, and for all others considered in *The Edges of Education*, glimpses of light can be detected in even the darkest of places. Indeed, darkness can open doors to a deeper, more nuanced and honest understanding of ourselves: our strengths and weaknesses, our connections with others (past and present), our hopes for the future.

---

5 For discussions of the book by other scholars, see Allen (2017); Bojesen (2017); Chen (2017, 2020); Longa and Fortier (2020); Jackson (2022); Laverty (2020); O'Connell (2016); Peters (2017); Reveley (2018) and Sarauw (2017).

6 Under the influence of positive psychology (Seligman, 2002) and the new 'science' of happiness (Layard, 2005), a range of initiatives designed to enhance student well-being had been introduced in schools and other educational institutions. While the 'happiness turn' was strongly supported by many, others expressed serious reservations about some of the assumptions underpinning these developments. The overt linking of well-being with productivity and economic advancement in more recent years (New Zealand Productivity Commission, 2017; OECD Better Life Initiative, 2019) has only added to these concerns. For a range of critical perspectives on happiness, well-being and education, see Binkley (2011); Cigman (2012); Ecclestone and Hayes (2008); Ferguson (2007); Gibbs and Dean (2014); Guilherme and de Freitas (2017); Jackson (2022); Jackson and Bingham (2018); Miller (2008); Rappleye et al. (2020); Reveley (2016); Roberts (2022); Shaw and Taplin (2007); Spratt (2017); Suissa (2008) and Zembylas (2020).

The terms 'light' and 'darkness' are employed here in a symbolic and metaphorical sense, but they can also sometimes be applied in a literal manner. Schopenhauer (1966a), for instance, sees light as 'the condition for the most perfect kind of knowledge, and therefore of the most delightful of things' (p. 203). How we find what is delightful – what is good and beautiful and true – while also acknowledging the difficulties we face is very much an educational problem. Light finds its way through our struggles, often coming to us not as a blinding flash, but more gradually and intermittently, and in more subtle forms. We can detect glimmers of light without having to undergo a sudden and dramatic process of illuminating transformation. The path is seldom smoothly upwards and will often involve setbacks, compromises and uncertainty in knowing what we have achieved. The 'darkness' of existence remains, even where joy can be found, and will often intrude exactly when it is least expected or wanted. The writers examined in this book help us to see that this dark undercurrent is not an aberration; not something that can be quickly and easily 'fixed' or removed. Rather, despair is always there, even for those who are seemingly most happy, most content (Kierkegaard, 1989). It may be masked – by denial, by distraction or by ignorance – but it continues to exert a quiet influence over our lives. Looking more closely at despair is itself an educational task worth undertaking, though by no means an easy one. There is a sense also in which light and darkness can intermingle, creating shadowy spaces for educational investigation. We may approach these spaces – these situations, experiences, ways of understanding and being in the world – with trepidation, perhaps with fear, but also with curiosity and a desire to know more. The chapters that follow flesh out some of the pathways for exploring these spaces and for making sense of them when we inhabit them.

There is, this book argues, no 'cure' for the despair we experience, but there are ways to learn to live with and from our suffering. There is, among the thinkers considered in this book, a common recognition of the value of art in making life more bearable, in expressing what is within and in revealing enduring truths to us.[7] This is especially so for Leopardi – himself a great poet – but it is also the case for Unamuno (who was a fine novelist and short story writer as well as an erudite scholar) and for Schopenhauer (who was, in later life, highly regarded in European art circles).[8] In Maxine Greene's work, there was always a seamless integration of educational, philosophical and artistic concerns. Education

---

7 'Art' here can include painting, sculpture, music, poetry, prose and other expressions of human creativity. See further, Roberts and Freeman-Moir (2013).

8 See Unamuno (1996, 2000) and, on Schopenhauer's influence, Cross (2013), Solomon and Higgins (1996) and Vandenabeele (2012).

for Greene was very much an aesthetic process. Weil too was eclectic in her reading tastes and wanted to give literature and the arts a more central place in the curriculum. For some of the writers featured in this volume, a certain calming of the mind is seen as crucial. Schopenhauer speaks of the importance of developing a state of absorbed contemplation, allowing us to be delivered, even if only momentarily, from the agitation and suffering engendered by constant willing. Weil, likewise, places a premium on the cultivation of our capacity for attention. Attention requires humility and patience. We must, Weil argues, learn to listen and to wait. Only then do we open up the possibility of overcoming the persistent influence of moral gravity, allowing grace to intervene. For others – most notably, Unamuno – restlessness and uncertainty are themselves signs of hope, keeping us alert, awake and alive. From each of these figures, we can learn that it is possible to go on, while simultaneously acknowledging that life is difficult, sometimes terrifyingly so. What emerges is a more rounded and realistic portrait of what it means to be human and with this, a reconsideration of the nature, purpose and significance of education.

A few brief comments on the structure of the book are needed. As befits a work in a series devoted to complicated conversations, *The Edges of Education* can be seen as an attempt to engage in a difficult but rewarding dialogue with a number of deep thinkers: Leopardi, Schopenhauer, Unamuno, Weil and Greene. Other fictional figures – Cervantes' Don Quixote and Sancho Panza and Beauvoir's Regina and Fosca – also enter the conversation at different points.[9] The ideas advanced by these writers, and the lessons we can learn from their literary creations, remain timely and important. They speak to pressing problems in our present age, including educational concerns, albeit in ways that might not be immediately obvious. The book is thematically driven rather than chronologically organised. Leopardi and Schopenhauer appear first in the book because of what they have to say, not because they happen to have been born first, and Chapters 3, 4 and 5 do not follow a similar chronological order. The progression across the chapters is from a starting point of disarmingly frank pessimism towards a position of hope with uncertainty. Leopardi and Schopenhauer paint a very bleak picture of the human condition but, it will be suggested, this need not be disabling. For educationists in particular, the starkly 'negative' nature of their outlook on life provides an invitation to think again about why, how and what we should seek to know. These possibilities expand as the focus shifts to

---

9   On the theory behind the notion of a complicated conversation in curriculum studies, see Pinar (2012, 2015, 2023).

the work of Weil and Greene, who encourage us, as teachers and learners, to be open and attentive, to ourselves, to others and to the world around us. The movement in the direction of uncertain hope reaches its limit, in this book at least, with a consideration of what some see as the biggest mystery of all: death. Death, it will be argued, provides the ultimate companion throughout our educational lives, quietly accompanying us at every stage of our learning journey, exerting a hidden but powerful influence over almost every decision we make.

The book begins with a focus on the thought of Giacomo Leopardi, who spent most of his short life in the Italian town of Recanati in the first few decades of the nineteenth century. Leopardi is best known for his poetry, but he also wrote at length on philosophical, cultural and artistic matters. Many of his most important ideas are captured in the *Zibaldone* (Leopardi, 2014), a vast collection of his reflections on nature, history, literature and the human condition. With his father's library at his disposal, and tutors available to assist him in his learning, Leopardi immersed himself in the scholarship of his intellectual forebears. He took his commitment to study to the limits of human endurance. He read widely, in multiple languages. He developed great breadth and depth in understanding, but the long hours bent over a desk had damaging consequences for his already frail physical health. He died while still in his thirties, having led a lonely but highly productive existence. A troubling, provocative thinker, Leopardi has, to date, attracted little attention from educationists. Chapter 1 sets out to show why this gap in the educational literature is worth addressing. The chapter begins with a brief account of Leopardi's philosophical position on nature, reason and the inevitability of human unhappiness. This is followed by a more detailed discussion of the educational dimensions of his work. It is argued that while Leopardi's grim perspective on life may be off-putting for many, his honesty in describing the realities of existence can also be enabling and educative.

Arthur Schopenhauer, like Leopardi, is well known for his philosophical pessimism. At the heart of Schopenhauer's worldview is the concept of an all-powerful will. For Schopenhauer, the will is timeless and universal; it is present in we human beings and in all of nature. The will stands behind everything that happens: every experience, every event, every thought, feeling and action. We distinguish ourselves from other living creatures in our striving to know, but this too is an expression of the will; we sense that we are deficient in something, and we endeavour to address this. In doing so, however, we remain perpetually dissatisfied. As subjects of willing, filled with hopes and desires, we remain restless and unfulfilled; as soon as one want is met, another arises. At first glance, there appears to be little room for hope here. Schopenhauer does, however, identify several avenues for finding some relief from the suffering that is characteristic of human existence. One of these, considered at length in chapter 2, is via moments of absorbed contemplation, where we find ourselves temporarily free of the dictates of the individual will, seeing, as it were, with the 'clear eye of the world' (Schopenhauer, 1966a, p. 186). The chapter reflects on this idea in the light of Schopenhauer's wider philosophy and explores its educational implications.

Chapter 3 examines the work of the influential French philosopher and teacher, Simone Weil, focusing in particular on the ethical and educational dimensions of her thought. Weil's ethical theory is considered against the backdrop of pivotal events in her life and in relation to her practical proposals for political and pedagogical change. The significance of Weil's work for educationists lies in her unique interpretation of several philosophical concepts – gravity, decreation and grace – and in the emphasis she places on the development of attention, a notion elaborated in this chapter via the key themes of truth, beauty and love (Weil, 1997, 2001a). In common with other thinkers featured in this volume, Weil stresses the need to pay attention to individual human beings. She expresses concern over the mentality of 'the crowd' and tends to avoid abstract categories such as 'humanity' when addressing ethical questions (see Weil, 2001b). There is, however, an important social dimension to her work, captured neatly by her coupling of 'rights' with 'obligations', the latter of which she sees as more fundamental than the former. For Weil (2002), a right only becomes a right because of the corresponding obligation it implies. This shifts the focus away from our own wants and demands, toward the needs of others. We demonstrate our commitment to others not by way of grand words or gestures but through myriad small acts of attention, in educational environments and in the other spaces we inhabit in our daily lives.

Simone Weil was just 34 years old when she died. She wrote and taught in the first half of the twentieth century, her work reflecting the troubles of that time while also speaking to more permanent problems and themes. The brevity of her life can be contrasted with the longevity granted to another remarkable thinker: Maxine Greene. Greene made notable contributions to educational theory in the second half of the twentieth century but, like Weil, she continues to be widely read today.[10] Chapter 4 begins with some remarks

---

10 This is especially so for those who place themselves in the 'Continental' tradition of philosophical scholarship in education. For examples of work in this domain, see Baldacchino and Saeverot (2024).

on one of her most influential works, *Teacher as Stranger* (Greene, 1973), and considers what it might mean to reverse the two key terms in this title: that is, to see the 'stranger as teacher'. It is argued that we can learn from strangers in a range of different contexts, both fictional and real. Strangers who appear to be 'mad' can have a particularly unsettling, but potentially educative, effect on us, and there is no clearer illustration of this than the figure of Don Quixote in Cervantes' (2005) classic novel of that name. In the company of Miguel de Unamuno (1972), Franz Kafka (2012) and Joshua Dienstag (2006), this chapter reflects on Don Quixote's madness and the pedagogical features of the novel. Particular attention is paid to the relationship between the knight errant and his travelling companion, Sancho Panza. The last part of the chapter explores some of the implications of the 'stranger as teacher' idea for classroom environments.

Chapter 5 considers the ultimate 'limit' we all must face: our own death. Often regarded as one of the few certainties in life, and approached cautiously if at all in everyday conversation, death has, over the ages, served as an important theme for philosophical rumination. For Socrates, philosophy was seen as a form of preparation for death: in placing a premium on the development of reason while living, we move closer to the separation of the soul from the body that occurs when we die (Plato, 2003). For Socrates, as for the Epicureans and the Stoics, learning how to live well was seen as a matter of 'learning to die' (Hadot, 1995). This idea merits further theoretical exploration in education. Chapter 5 builds on the small but growing body of work by philosophers of education on death and dying. It pays particular attention to the idea of immortality, so central to ancient Greek and Roman thought and a vital component of many religious traditions. A belief in immortality continues to provide comfort for many people today, not just as they contemplate their own deaths but also as they think about what has happened to loved ones who have passed away before them. For others, however, the question of immortality is far more complicated and difficult. Miguel de Unamuno had a deep longing to live on, but the voice of critical reason kept prodding away at him, telling him that this idea was ridiculous. In this chapter, the tragic tension identified by Unamuno (1972) – between faith and feeling on the one hand and science and logic on the other – serves as the starting point for a more extended discussion of immortality in education. The chapter shows that the striving for immortality that is so prominent in Unamuno's work is also evident, in more subtle and symbolic ways, in our educational endeavours. Drawing on Simone de Beauvoir's (1992) novel, *All Men Are Mortal,* and reflecting on recent developments in computing, biotechnology and surveillance, it is argued that not all forms of immortality are desirable. The last part of the chapter advances an alternative view on education and immortality, emphasising the importance of uncertainty, humility and openness in facing death, both as a subject for inquiry and as a reality we all must confront.

A few final remarks on the limitations of this volume may be helpful. *The Edges of Education* does not set out to provide definitive portraits of any one of the intellectual figures who serve as prompts for discussion throughout. With the exception of the chapter on Weil, biographical details are kept to a minimum, and the ideas under examination represent only a limited sampling of what each of these writers has to offer. There is no one problem that lies behind the story being told here; instead, the book responds, via a series of thematically linked chapters, to a range of related questions and concerns.[11] The argument emerges not in a systematic fashion but in the form of interconnected threads, more readily identifiable, perhaps, by the end of the book than at the beginning. This is a work in education, not in philosophy or politics or literary criticism. Acknowledgement is made of previous educational scholarship relevant to the content of each chapter, but those with more specialised interests in particular areas will want to complement what they find in these pages with other sources.[12] Consistent with the position signalled earlier in this Introduction, and reinforced throughout the book, *The Edges of Education* is incomplete and uncertain in the conclusions it draws.[13] Those seeking firmer

---

11 Several of the key concerns have been prefigured in this Introduction: a tendency toward excessive certainties (and a corresponding disregard for the importance of uncertainty); an obsession with measurement and performance (and a marginalising of those aspects of educational experience that do not conform to this logic); an unreflective favouring of 'positive' perspectives on the human condition (accompanied by a reluctance to examine the role of suffering and despair in our formation); and the heavy emphasis on the benefits of education (with a concomitant neglect of the more troubling and unsettling features of educational life).

12 Suggestions for further reading will often be found in the footnotes included with each chapter. Footnotes will also, at times, add supplementary points to the main text, with the aim of clarifying or extending what has been said without disrupting the flow of the argument. The hope is that they will be seen as an important part of the book, complementing the rest of the material, while also opening up possibilities for continuing dialogue and scholarship on a range of themes and thinkers.

13 There is, deliberately, no 'Conclusion' chapter. The book 'ends' with the chapter on death, as this seems most appropriate given everything said in leading up to that point and as a reflection of the way life unfolds.

answers to the questions posed may be disappointed. It is hoped, nonetheless, that curious, patient readers will find something new and worthwhile in this volume. *The Edges of Education* pulls aside a veil that often covers educational inquiry, allowing a glimpse into some of the more unsettling but also liberating aspects of teaching and learning.[14] It does so via engagement with the work of a number of thinkers who feature only rarely in the educational literature but who arguably warrant greater attention. It places difficult subjects – death, despair and madness, for instance – more squarely on the table for educational consideration. This book is intended to foster further reflection on, and exploration of, the spaces we find at the edges of education: inner territories that can leave us feeling shaken and disturbed but also full of restless anticipation for the potentially rewarding pedagogical journey that lies ahead.

References

Allen, A. (2017). Review of *Happiness, hope, and despair: Rethinking the role of education*. *Policy Futures in Education*, *15*(6), 803–804.

Baldacchino, J. & Saeverot, H. (Eds.). (2024). *The Bloomsbury handbook of Continental philosophy of education*. Bloomsbury.

Beauvoir, S. de (1948). *The ethics of ambiguity* (B. Frechtman, Trans.). Citadel Press.

Beauvoir, S. de (1992). *All men are mortal* (L. M. Friedman, Trans.). W. W. Norton.

Binkley, S. (2011). Happiness, positive psychology and the program of neoliberal governmentality. *Subjectivity*, *4*, 371–394.

Bojesen, E. (2017). Review of *Happiness, hope, and despair: Rethinking the role of education*. *Educational Philosophy and Theory*, *49*(14), 1461–1462.

Cervantes, M. de (2005). *Don Quixote* (E. Grossman, Trans.). Vintage.

Chen, R.H. (2017). Review of *Happiness, hope, and despair: Rethinking the role of education*. *Educational Philosophy and Theory*, *49*(14), 1452–1454.

Chen, R.H. (2020). "To be born of hardship" and "To die from comfort!". *Studies in Philosophy and Education*, *39*(5), 569–571.

Cigman, R. (2012). We need to talk about well-being. *Research Papers in Education*, *27*(4), 449–462.

Cross, S. (2013). *Schopenhauer's encounter with Indian thought: Representation and will and their Indian parallels*. University of Hawaii Press.

---

14 Teaching and learning can be 'liberating' – in the specific sense being employed here – both in terms of what we are released from (e.g. the shackles of certainty) and exposed to (e.g. new forms of sublime experience). This connects with the idea of 'limits' and 'possibilities' signalled in the subtitle of this book.

D'Olimpio, L. (2024). *The necessity of aesthetic education: The place of the arts on the curriculum.* Bloomsbury.

Dienstag, J. F. (2006). *Pessimism: Philosophy, ethic, spirit.* Princeton University Press.

Ecclestone, K. & Hayes, D. (2008). *The dangerous rise of therapeutic education.* Routledge.

Ferguson, I. (2007). Neoliberalism, happiness and wellbeing. *International Socialism: A Quarterly Review of Socialist Theory,* 117, 1–16.

Gibbs, P. & Dean, A. (2014). Troubling the notion of satisfied students. *Higher Education Quarterly,* 68(4), 416–431.

Greene, M. (1973). *Teacher as stranger.* Wadsworth.

Guilherme, A. & de Freitas, A. L. S. (2017). 'Happiness education': A pedagogical-political commitment. *Policy Futures in Education,* 15(1), 6–19.

Hadot, P. (1995). *Philosophy as a way of life.* (M. Chase, Trans.). Blackwell.

Jackson, L. (2022). *Beyond virtue: The politics of educating emotions.* Cambridge University Press.

Jackson, L. & Bingham, C. (2018). Reconsidering happiness in the context of social justice education. *Interchange: A Quarterly Review of Education,* 49, 217–229.

Kafka, F. (2012). *A hunger artist and other stories* (J. Crick, Trans.). Oxford University Press.

Kierkegaard, S. (1985). *Philosophical fragments* (H. V. Hong & E. H. Hong, Trans.). Princeton, NJ: Princeton University Press.

Kierkegaard, S. (1989). *The sickness unto death* (A. Hannay, Trans.). Penguin.

Kierkegaard, S. (2009). *Concluding unscientific postscript* (A. Hannay, Trans.). Cambridge University Press.

Laverty, M.J. (2020). Making space for irony. *Studies in Philosophy and Education,* 39(5), 559–563.

Layard, R. (2005). *Happiness: Lessons from a new science.* Penguin.

Leopardi, G. (2014). *Zibaldone* (M. Caesar & F. D'Intino, Eds.). Farrar, Straus and Giroux.

Longa, R. & Fortier, N. (2020). "Restlessness, agitation, and passion": Rethinking the role of narrative in education. *Studies in Philosophy and Education,* 39(5), 565–567.

Miller, A. (2008). A critique of positive psychology – or 'the new science of happiness'. *Journal of Philosophy of Education,* 42(3–4), 591–608.

New Zealand Productivity Commission (2017). *New models of tertiary education: Final Report.* <www.productivity.govt.nz/inquiry-content/tertiary-education>

O'Connell, T. (2016). Review of *Happiness, hope, and despair: Rethinking the role of education.* *Teachers College Record.* <http://www.tcrecord.org>

OECD Better Life Initiative (2019). *Measuring well-being and progress.* OECD Statistics and Data Directorate.

Peters, M. A. (2017). Review of *Happiness, hope, and despair: Rethinking the role of education.* *New Zealand Journal of Educational Studies,* 52, 185–187.

Pinar, W. F. (2012). *What is curriculum theory?* 2nd edition. Routledge.

Pinar, W. F. (2015). *Educational experience as lived: Knowledge, history, alterity – The selected writings of William F. Pinar.* Routledge.

Pinar, W. F. (2023). *A praxis of presence in curriculum theory: Advancing* currere *against cultural crises in education.* Routledge.

Plato (2003). *The last days of Socrates* (H. Tredennick & H. Tarrant, Trans.). Penguin.

Postman, N. & Weingartner, D. (1971). *Teaching as a subversive activity.* Penguin.

Rappleye, J., Komatsu, H., Uchida, Y., Krys, K. & Markus, H. (2020). "Better policies for better lives"?: Constructive critique of the OECD's (mis)measure of student well-being. *Journal of Education Policy*, 35(2), 258–282.

Reveley, J. (2016). Neoliberal meditations: How mindfulness training medicalizes education and responsibilizes young people. *Policy Futures in Education*, 14(4), 497–511.

Reveley, J. (2018). Embracing the humanistic vision: Recurrent themes in Peter Roberts' recent writings. *Educational Philosophy and Theory*, 50(3), 312–321.

Roberts, P. (2016). *Happiness, hope, and despair: Rethinking the role of education*. Peter Lang.

Roberts, P. (2022). *Performativity, politics and education: From policy to philosophy*. Brill.

Roberts, P. & Freeman-Moir, J. (2013). *Better worlds: Education, art, and utopia*. Lexington Books.

Sarauw, L. L. (2017). Review of *Happiness, hope, and despair: Rethinking the role of education*. *Educational Philosophy and Theory*, 49(14), 1455–1457.

Schopenhauer, A. (1966a). *The world as will and representation*, vol. 1 (E. F. Payne, Trans.). Dover.

Schopenhauer, A. (1966b). *The world as will and representation*, vol. 2 (E. F. Payne, Trans.). Dover.

Seligman, M. E. P. (2002). *Authentic happiness: Using the new positive psychology to realize your potential for lasting fulfillment*. Random House.

Shaw, I. & Taplin, S. (2007). Happiness: A sociological critique of Layard. *Journal of Mental Health*, 16(3), 359–373.

Solomon, R. C. & Higgins, K. M. (1996). *A short history of philosophy*. Oxford University Press.

Spratt, J. (2017). *Wellbeing, equity and education: A critical analysis of policy discourses of wellbeing in schools*. Springer.

Suissa, J. (2008). Lessons from a new science? On teaching happiness in schools. *Journal of Philosophy of Education*, 42(3–4), 575–590.

Unamuno, M. de (1972). *The tragic sense of life in men and nations* (A. Kerrigan, Trans.). Princeton University Press.

Unamuno, M. de (1996). *Abel Sanchez and other stories* (A. Kerrigan, Trans.). Regnery Publishing.

Unamuno, M. de (2000). *Mist: A tragicomic novel* (W. Fite, Trans.). University of Illinois Press.

Vandenabeele, B. (2012). Introduction: Arthur Schopenhauer – The man and his work. In B. Vandenabeele (Ed.), *A companion to Schopenhauer* (pp. 1–8). Oxford: Blackwell.

Weil, S. (1997). *Gravity and grace* (A. Wills, Trans.). Bison Books.

Weil, S. (2001a). *Waiting for God* (E. Craufurd, Trans.). Perennial Classics.

Weil, S. (2001b). *Oppression and liberty*. Routledge.

Weil, S. (2002). *The need for roots* (A. Wills, Trans.). Routledge Classics.

Zembylas, M. (2020). (Un)happiness and social justice education: Ethical, political and pedagogic lessons. *Ethics and Education*, 15(1), 18–32.

· 1 ·

NATURE, REASON AND EDUCATION: LEARNING WITH LEOPARDI

In his native Italy, Giacomo Leopardi (1798–1837) is revered by many as a great poet – an heir to Dante – and a brilliant scholar.[1] Leopardi has left his mark on the work of a number of influential European thinkers, including Arthur Schopenhauer, Friedrich Nietzsche, Miguel de Unamuno, Walter Benjamin and Antonio Negri.[2] In the English-speaking world, he has, with some notable exceptions, been largely ignored.[3] The relative neglect of Leopardi in

---

1   See Valiunas (2022, p. 28).
2   Schopenhauer saw Leopardi as a kindred intellectual spirit and acknowledged him directly in the second volume of his magnum opus, *The World as Will and Representation* (Schopenhauer, 1966b, p. 588). Nietzsche (1997) draws on Leopardi in the second of his *Untimely Meditations* (Nietzsche, 1997). The Italian's influence is also evident in Nietzsche's idea of eternal recurrence, as developed in *The Gay Science* (Nietzsche, 1974). Unamuno refers repeatedly to Leopardi in *The Tragic Sense of Life in Men and Nations* (Unamuno, 1972). On the links between Benjamin and Leopardi, see Baker (2006). Antonio Negri, a significant figure in contemporary political philosophy, devoted one of his early books to Leopardi and has continued to stress his importance in later discussions with other scholars (see Negri, 2015; Negri & Casarino, 2008).
3   The best-known exception is arguably the Irish playwright and Nobel laureate, Samuel Beckett (see Bouchard, 1999; Caselli, 1996; Cauchi-Santoro, 2015). The 'English-speaking world' in this context refers to those countries where English is the first or dominant language. It is recognised that a number of the European thinkers who have engaged with Leopardi's ideas have been fluent in English as well as in their first language.

the United Kingdom, the United States, Canada and Australasia during the twentieth century can be partly explained by the dearth of written material available in English translation. With the publication of an English version of the complete *Zibaldone di pensieri* in 2014, a crucial gap in the existing literature on and by this remarkable and troubling figure has been filled. Running to over 2500 printed pages, the *Zibaldone* (Leopardi, 2014) is a 'hodgepodge' of reflections from the notebooks Leopardi kept throughout his adult life. The themes addressed in the work range widely over philosophy, religion, politics, language, literature, art and culture. The *Zibaldone* is not a systematic treatise, but neither is it merely a random assortment of opinions and observations.[4] Leopardi could be contrary, cutting and curt. At times, he appears to be either lashing out or laughing at the world. Yet he was also a supremely subtle and sensitive writer. His prose is exemplary in its clarity and elegance. There is a unity to his thought, with a regular circling back to key ideas. There is also a strong undercurrent of sadness and loneliness in the pages of the *Zibaldone*. Leopardi is a key contributor to the pessimistic tradition (Dienstag, 2006) and his courage in facing up to the despair of the human condition is what some have admired most in his work.[5]

Leopardi's significance for educationists lies not just in the ideas he expounded but in the manner through which he communicates. As Michael Caesar and Franco D'Intino point out in their Introduction to the *Zibaldone*, Leopardi's voice 'truly fascinates and educates us, because it is never a "specialist" who is talking, but an ancient *teacher* who thinks *poetically*' (Caesar & D'Intino, 2014, p. xiv).[6] While Leopardi makes some direct remarks on pedagogical matters in the *Zibaldone*, he does not offer a comprehensive 'theory'

---

4   In this sense, the 'hodgepodge' label is somewhat misleading. There is an immediacy to Leopardi's writing, with fewer self-imposed authorial barriers than might be expected in a more traditional philosophical text, but the *Zibaldone*, when read holistically, does not lack coherence. In the *Zibaldone*, there are variations in rhetorical strategies and registers across different genres and subject areas (Mirra, 2016). But despite the diversity of themes and styles, the *Zibaldone* is unified by a desire to 'establish a dialogue with an absent interlocutor', who could be 'an ancient philosopher, a contemporary scholar, or a future reader'; this means that the work is 'positioned out of time, at a crossroads between past, present, and future' (Ferri, 2018, p. 15).

5   As will be discussed later in this chapter, this is particularly true of Schopenhauer and Unamuno. Schopenhauer's philosophical position is outlined in some detail in chapter 2 of this book. Unamuno features in chapter 4 and is a pivotal figure in chapter 5.

6   Indeed, it is possible to see the process Leopardi adopted in writing the *Zibaldone* as a form of self-education (Cori, 2016).

of education. Instead, he allows us, as readers, to fashion our own educational paths, having first planted some seeds of doubt. Leopardi unsettles and disturbs, as any good teacher should.[7] His presence lingers, long after we have first encountered a passage in his work, keeping us slightly off-balance as we attempt to make sense of ourselves and our surroundings. Leopardi provides not solace or support but, perhaps against his own inclinations, a kind of solidarity. Here we find a fellow human sufferer; someone who peered into the abyss of existence and refused to look away. Leopardi's educational journey was very much his own, as for each of us ours must be too. But there is a sense of connection that can be forged with this Italian poet that transcends some of the usual boundaries of time and space. He is, it will be argued in this chapter, worthy of our attention as teachers and learners, even if we may not always like what he helps us to see. We can, if we are sufficiently well prepared, learn with Leopardi. In the discussion that follows, some of the principal aspects of Leopardi's worldview are articulated and the educational implications of his ideas are explored.

Nature, Reason and Unhappiness: Leopardi on the Human Condition

From a Leopardian point of view, our human condition is fundamentally tragic. In this sense, Leopardi shares much in common with a number of other thinkers examined in this volume. As human beings, we are doomed to be unhappy. We are 'essentially wretched because our nature makes it so, and cannot change' (Leopardi, 2014, p. 47). Leopardi sees our unhappiness as proof of our immortality. Among living creatures, he points out, we alone are capable of contemplating suicide. The instinct to survive is present throughout the animal kingdom but we – with our perpetually unfulfilled desires, our dissatisfaction with the present and our ability to imagine the worst in the future – can ponder the possibility of not existing. Among the ancients, some who found themselves in a state of despair killed themselves because they saw their misfortunes as peculiar to them – as individual, accidental and exceptional. From Leopardi's perspective, however, discouragement with life – a sense that it is a burden rather than a good – is 'our fate and inevitable in our species' (p. 271). We may be lords over planet Earth, but we cannot enjoy the perfection

---

7 Or at least any good teacher of adults. With children, the idea of 'teaching as unsettling' must be applied in an age-appropriate and context-sensitive manner.

of our being. So long as we live like other animals, we can attain a measure of happiness, but the moment we reflect upon 'the emptiness of things and the illusoriness and nothingness of these same natural pleasures' this happiness disappears (p. 63). Thinking corrupts us.[8] Already corrupted, we can nonetheless grasp that 'small pleasures reward us better than any other' (p. 63). We see less discontent in children than in adults and in those who are illiterate compared with those who are educated (p. 63). The more fully we develop and exercise our distinctive human capacity for critical thought, the more miserable we become.

Reason, Leopardi suggests, 'is the enemy of all greatness' (p. 15). Nature is great but reason is small (pp. 15, 42). Religion provides a form of reconciliation between nature and reason by encouraging us to love what is invisible (i.e. a deity) and by making seemingly irrational actions and attitudes seem rational (e.g. sacrificing one's own pleasure to the service of God and feeling scorn in the face of death). If we do not have religion, we must turn to words, to art. If greatness is to be achieved in the arts, one cannot be governed principally by reason; it is essential to be guided by illusions. Great deeds are performed not in accordance with order and rationality but arise, as exceptional events, from disorder. Greatness emerges as something disruptive, something extraordinary. But what counts as exceptional can also differ from one era to another. Leopardi maintains that in today's world,[9] far less is needed to create the same effect that Diogenes had in ancient Greece (p. 44). To be seen as mad in the Athens of his time, Diogenes needed to perform extreme deeds; he had to be truly unique, truly strange, in a manner and to a degree that would not be necessary in the contemporary world. Our expectations, not only of ourselves but also of the art we create, have narrowed. Hence, 'if someone calls his work a tragedy, the public expects what is usually understood by a tragedy, and if it finds something altogether different it laughs at it' (p. 45). To be truly original, Leopardi contends, 'you need to break, violate, scorn, completely abandon customs and habits and the idea of names, genres, etc., accepted by everyone' (p. 45). This is, as he points out, not easy to do. Courage is required, and those who risk it all in this way can quickly find themselves in a lonely and precarious position.

---

8   In making this point, Leopardi acknowledges Rousseau.
9   He was writing, it must be remembered, in the first half of the nineteenth century. It seems likely, however, that if Leopardi was with us now, he would make the same claim – perhaps even more emphatically.

For Leopardi, reason is not the liberating force the modern age promised it would be. Reason inhibits and constrains, it creates suffering and pain, and it prevents us from living on good terms with ourselves. This view presupposes a division between what is 'natural' and what is 'rational' that would itself not have been necessary in our more distant past. But nature is, so to speak, still there, still 'with us' now even as reason rallies against her. Leopardi may live in the modern age, but he can still turn to nature in making sense of himself and his purpose. As an artist, he is clear about what drives him. He is adamant that nature provides the inspiration for greatness; reason holds us back. Reason, in its rigidity, repels and separates; it stands opposed to beauty. Subjected to the cold gaze of reason, everything in this world ultimately becomes 'ugly and barren' (p. 43). For Leopardi, a poet 'must not only imitate and depict nature perfectly but also imitate and depict it naturally' (p. 22). A great poet like Dante uses words to tell a story, with exquisite descriptions but without having to draw the reader's attention to every little detail. Dante allows us to see what is there without having to reveal the work he has put into creating his art. Most 'useful' works provide only indirect pleasure, showing how it can be obtained; poetry brings pleasure to us immediately (p. 23). If prose is to be truly beautiful, it must have a certain poetic quality. Technical terms, of the kind that may be fashionable in contemporary times, can destroy the 'softness and malleability' we find in the ancients (p. 35).[10] The language of prose can, when severed from its roots in antiquity, become 'geometric, arid, emaciated, hard, dry ...' (p. 36). The prose Leopardi cherishes has a vibrant freshness; it is 'soft, healthy, rosy, luxuriant ...' with a 'florid fleshiness' (p. 36).

While Leopardi draws our attention to the limits of reason, and to its damaging consequences for us as human beings, this does not mean he abandons a commitment to truth.[11] In many respects, the entire *Zibaldone* represents a prolonged quest to discover truths, palatable and unpalatable, through the act of writing. Indeed, Leopardi's monumental contribution as a poet can be conceived as a desperate attempt to not only reveal deeper truths behind everyday appearances but to *live truthfully* – that is, in a manner that was true to himself.

---

10 Again, while these views were formed in the early 1800s, it is not difficult to imagine Leopardi wanting to reinforce them in observing twenty-first century life. In both the arts and the sciences, there is now greater specialisation than ever before, with ways of speaking and making sense of the world that are often only comprehensible to those immersed in a given paradigm within a specific field of inquiry.

11 For a philosophical, literary and educational consideration of the limits of reason, see Roberts and Saeverot (2018).

Leopardi was, in Kierkegaard's (2009) terms, very much an *individual*, notwithstanding the links he makes between his own endeavours and those of his ancient forebears. Leopardi cannot stop himself from remembering, but he is also painfully aware of what this means for his sense of well-being. He observes that drunkenness tends to be associated with joy rather than melancholy and provides a twofold explanation for this. First, 'melancholy derives from truth, not falsehood, and drunkenness causes us to forget the truth, *and only from that forgetfulness can joy be born*' (Leopardi, 2014, p. 98, emphasis in the original). Second, 'men in the state of nature … were meant to be happy and abandon themselves to illusions and to see and feel them as if they were living and bodily presences' (p. 98). Memory, in the form of conscious, deliberate recollection and reflection, is thus a kind of curse; it condemns us to unhappiness, and it leaves us with a deep sadness that never quite disappears. Memory awakens us; it has a sobering rather than inebriating effect. We may find temporary relief in moments where we, as it were, 'forget ourselves', but we invariably return to the state of despair that underpins all critical, reasoning life.

Leopardi argues that there is 'no memory without attention' (p. 789). To illustrate this point, he asks us to imagine a situation with two people, both of whom have the same capacity for memory, but who, when encountering an accident, differ in the attention they pay to it. One attends closely; the other does not. If, after a period of time has elapsed, we question them both, the former 'will remember it as if it were happening now, the latter as if it had not happened at all' (p. 789). This may seem obvious, but it is an observation with important educational implications. If we want to remember, deliberate, careful development of the ability to pay attention is often crucial. Leopardi teaches us, however, that we may *not* always want to remember, and this raises questions for those committed to teaching, learning and the acquisition of knowledge. It should be noted, moreover, that Leopardi distinguishes between two different types of attention. He refers to one as voluntary (or spiritual), the other as involuntary (or material). The first of these is only possible through habitual application of our capacity to pay attention. This, for Leopardi, explains why those with thoughtful minds generally have good memories; for them, even small details can be recalled, because they are well practised in the art of paying attention. Attention of the second kind arises in situations where we experience something in a particularly intense way, where the impression is such that we cannot ignore what has occurred. We are, in these instances, 'forced' to pay attention. This means 'susceptible and imaginative spirits' may have excellent memories, even if they are not normally attentive, because 'everything makes a proportionately greater impression on them' than it does on others (p. 790). Our memories from childhood are often more vivid and enduring than those from adulthood because at that stage in our lives, all impressions have a more extraordinary character.

Leopardi sees only some forms of memory as pleasant. Experiences where 'thought grows uncertain' – via our reading of poetry, for instance – can be pleasurable. Scenes of domestic and rural life, in painting and in literature, can be 'gratifying, agreeable, elegant' (p. 805). This is because they 'are commonplace things that are known and belong to everyone' (p. 805). Much that arises through memory can, however, be troubling, unsettling and unpleasant. Leopardi shows, in the *Zibaldone* and in the example furnished by his own life, that too much thinking of a certain kind – informed by relentless reason and reflection – can be distressing and debilitating. Moving toward the opposite end of the spectrum – that is, not thinking at all, to the extent that this is possible – can be beneficial for us. Leopardi suggests that the period where we begin to approach sleep can be pleasurable. It is, he stresses, not sleep itself that provides the pleasure but the torpor associated with it – the process of forgetting, where we find temporary respite from our usual 'desires, fears, hopes, passions of every kind' (p. 805). Drunkenness, with its tendency to promote forgetfulness, has sometimes been seen in a similar light. The element of forgetting is also what gives us pleasure in moments of great joy. Such moments will always be fleeting, but they can help in sustaining us. Intense joy can be experienced when 'the mind … relinquishes itself, and becomes altogether torpid on the one hand, and revives on the other' (p. 805). Joy is often sought through arousing the passions, through stimulating them as much as possible. Seen in this light, joy emerges when we remind ourselves of what we are capable of doing, of feeling and experiencing. But Leopardi's work suggests that such efforts tend in the wrong direction. It is through forgetting – through the 'total quietue of the passions' – that we find pleasure (p. 805).

The experience of being busy or distracted can also serve as something of a shield in warding off the worst effects of the unhappiness that plagues us all. As human beings, we are inevitably frustrated in our pursuit of happiness; we can attain it only fleetingly, and when we do, it is never enough. We want more, and we want what we cannot have. Activity distracts us from the unhappiness to which we all return. 'The happiest creature possible', Leopardi claims, 'is the one who is most distracted from the mind's tendency toward absolute happiness' (p. 334). We find greater happiness not by seeking it but by avoiding thinking about it, and about ourselves. A busy person, then, will tend to be less unhappy than one who has nothing to do. For both those who are busy and those who are not, it remains the case that 'life itself is an ill', but for the former group this thought will be less prominent and persistent (p. 1718). When such thoughts do occur, they will, among those who are busy or distracted, pass more quickly. For Leopardi, this suggests that having 'more feeling, more awareness of life' makes our time here that much harder, that much more miserable. Our unhappiness is increased when we consider how long life – and therefore our suffering – will be. 'To feel life less and to make it seem shorter', Leopardi asserts, 'is the greatest good, or rather the greatest reduction of ill and unhappiness which man can obtain' (p. 1719). This is why boredom, a state that in itself is not suffering or illness, can often bring unhappiness. Boredom is simply 'life itself fully felt, experienced, recognized, life fully present to the individual and taking him over' (p. 1719). The conclusion Leopardi draws from this reasoning is predictably grim: if life is 'simply an ill', then 'not to live, or to live less, whether in duration or in intensity, is simply a good, or a lesser ill' (p. 1719).

This does not mean life, having been granted to us, needs to be experienced without hope. Leopardi's position on hope is intimately linked with his views on happiness and unhappiness. We have seen that, for Leopardi, lasting happiness is not possible. We keep seeking happiness, but we continue to fall short in doing so. Pleasure is always something that is in the future, not in the present (p. 396). This provides part of the explanation for the hope some have that their name and fame will live on for posterity. This desire may sustain us to some degree, but it rests on an illusion. As Leopardi points out, human beings tend to want the pleasure of glory while they are living, not just once they have gone. More than this, though, if glory is achieved here and now, we find that it is not what we expected, not as we had hoped. We are not merely dissatisfied; we feel as if we have achieved nothing. Hope for lasting glory, beyond death, is, as it were, compensation for the inevitable sense of failure – of dissatisfaction and unhappiness – we experience while living. Happiness remains a necessary goal, and as human beings we continue to work towards this. Without hope, we could not do so. But when hope finds no home in this life, it 'finally finds a place beyond it' (p. 397). This illusion is more prevalent among those who are exceptional ('great men', as Leopardi refers to them), for others – those who 'know less about things or reason less and are less logical' – suffer only 'partial' disappointments; they can 'continue to hope within the bounds of their life' (p. 397). Those who grasp the futility of life, and quickly realise that lasting happiness cannot be experienced here in Earth, cling with a kind of necessary desperation to the only illusion left open to them: hope that their lives will come to matter, permanently, after they are gone. This hope may be necessary, but Leopardi is unflinching in his assessment of our prospects: even if in death we could exist forever in the glory we have achieved, our fame 'would seem to us, as our present fame does, completely insipid, and empty, and unable to satisfy or procure any other than future pleasure' (p. 397).

Despair is often construed as a state of mind in which we are without hope. But it is, as has been argued elsewhere (Roberts, 2016), precisely in conditions of despair that hope gains its meaning and significance. When all appears to be well, when we are apparently happy and content, with few worries, there is little need for hope. Hope under such circumstances may seem frivolous, empty, lacking in substance. It is when we are most desperate, at seemingly our lowest ebb, that hope, as it were 'comes into its own'. When we are staring into the abyss, hope becomes not just an interesting abstract idea but an existential necessity. It is only then, when we feel all is lost, or about to be lost, that we can truly understand what hope means and appreciate why we must cling on to it as fragile, flawed human beings. Despair is not so much 'without' hope as 'in' hope, and the reverse is also true: hope is in despair. Leopardi knew this. As he puts it, 'despair itself would not subsist without hope, and man would not despair if he did not hope' (Leopardi, 2014, p. 718). Despair, he maintains, is at its weakest among those who have already reached old age, with death approaching and the trials of life behind them. It is at its strongest in the young; in those who, lacking in experience but full of hope, still have their whole lives ahead of them. The experience of despair can also be particularly vivid for those who are ordinarily carefree, basking in the glow of their good fortune. There is, for these individuals, a sense of shock that must be absorbed, a startling disruption to the normal state of affairs. A person of this frame of mind, when facing despair for the first time, can feel disoriented, anxious and fearful. As Leopardi observes, '[t]he despair of the man who is ordinarily happy is terrifying' (p. 718). Yet, even in a state of utter desperation, there remains hope, 'in the depths of the heart' (p. 718). Despair itself is 'born from, and maintained by, the hope … to suffer less by neither hoping nor desiring anything more' (p. 718). We seek to persuade ourselves that this will allow us to find more enjoyment or freedom, to gain more control over our lives, with greater security and more of a 'nothing left to lose' attitude (p. 718). If we feel our despair is complete, at its most extreme and across the whole of life, we may nonetheless retain a certain hope: 'the hope of taking revenge on fortune or on oneself', perhaps even 'the hope of enjoying despair itself, the very agitation, the inner life, the powerful feelings … it arouses' (p. 718). Hope is essential if we are to live, and we can keep living in despair because despair 'contains hope' (p. 718).

Leopardi offers a helpful analogy (one he admits has been advanced before) in explaining his view of life. He compares the experience of living with the act of lying down on a hard bed. We feel uncomfortable and restless, tossing and turning, attempting to smooth out or soften the surface in order to rest and sleep. Eventually, after enduring physical discomfort all night, the time arrives to get up, and we do not feel rested at all. Life is just like this, with a restlessness that can never be assuaged and discontentment that cannot ever be fully addressed, despite our many efforts to make ourselves feel more comfortable, less unhappy. Death finally arrives, without our hopes having come to anything (p. 1759). Leopardi pushes this argument even further, noting that habitual unhappiness eventually 'extinguishes … in the most sensitive soul all imagination, every property of feeling, all vitality, activity, and strength, and almost every faculty' (p. 1760). This can lead to a sense of indifference toward the self, constituting, in its extreme form, 'a perfect death for the mind and its faculties' (p. 1760). We all live in despair but this form of 'calm desperation' is very different from the 'furious' kind, where there remains a trace of hope or at least desire (p. 1761). 'A man who is not interested in himself', Leopardi believes, 'is not capable of being interested in anything' (p. 1760). Nothing can help; not music, or poetry, or the beauty of nature. The events of the world and the experiences of others, including those closest to us, become a matter of indifference. If we desire nothing for ourselves, and have lost all love for ourselves, we become no good for anyone else. We cannot cry over ourselves, but neither can we feel or show compassion for others. At this point, hope is gone, and life is over.

Leopardi and Education: Teaching, Learning and Experience

What does Leopardi have to offer educational theory and practice? His direct statements on pedagogical matters provide a start in addressing this question. His views on teaching occupy only a small fraction of the total contents of the *Zibaldone*, but they are intriguing nonetheless. He notes, for example, that those who are specialists in a particular field or discipline are often not best placed to teach it. If two people are selected – one who is an expert in a given subject area and another 'whose mastery of the topic is somewhat less' – it is the latter who is usually better than the former at explaining the ideas to others (p. 653). The expert – the person who has all the knowledge at his or her fingertips – will want to communicate clearly but often struggles to do so. Specialisation may be much greater now than it was in Leopardi's time, but even then, there were complaints about 'the obscurity with which those who profess their disciplines ... expound them' (p. 653). In professing a discipline, it was already recognised that one is essentially 'speaking or writing for professionals' (p. 653). Leopardi suggests that while this may be appropriate in some fields of study, it ought not to be the case for other forms of knowledge – such as philosophy – that should be 'for everyone' (p. 653). One does not have to be eminent in a discipline to teach it well, but other qualities are necessary. Leopardi argues that the 'principal talent of a good teacher and the most useful one is not excellence in a particular doctrine, but excellence in knowing how to communicate it' (p. 654). Among those who are most learned in their fields, there are few who are capable of recalling how their ideas developed; how they gained the knowledge they have in their subject area (p. 654). Most specialists thus have a poor appreciation of what it must be like for the novice who is just beginning to acquire knowledge in their field. Those who do possess 'the imagination needed for the power to communicate' are 'geniuses' (p. 654).

Leopardi also considers the relationship between teaching and experience. He argues that while the young are 'never persuaded of the truth prior to having experienced it', parents and care givers are equally adamant that in their case, the teaching they offer can stand in for experience (p. 862). It is as if those charged with teaching the young forget that they too were once children and adolescents, who had to learn things for themselves before they could be convinced by others. Just as young people see themselves, individually, as exceptions to the rule, so too do those who are older (and who have pedagogical responsibilities) often act as if the situations with which they are dealing are different from the norm. They believe words and instructions will somehow work now, even if they have been inadequate in the past. The push-and-pull between young and old is thus doomed to keep repeating itself, and there is a perpetual process of forgetting what has been learned from experience. The case of Leopardi himself is fascinating when examined in this light. His own parents imposed severe restrictions on him, and much of the knowledge he gained was from books rather than the wider world. He barely ventured beyond his hometown in Italy, but the scope of his scholarly erudition was vast. His experiences with women were limited, and problematic, but this did not stop him from offering his opinions on the strengths and weaknesses of both sexes.[12] He rebelled against his parents in some respects – forging his own path as

---

12 For one perspective on Leopardi's troubling attitude towards women, see Rosengarten (2012).

a poet, for example – but in other ways he remained repressed and subservient. He did learn from his experiences, but he perhaps did not fully appreciate how limited and limiting those experiences had been. And the lessons he acquired from life often failed to bring about any change in his behaviour. He knew from experience how damaging to his health his obsessive scholarly efforts had been, and yet he could not, for the most part, stop himself from continuing down this destructive path.

The deeper significance of Leopardi's thought for education lies in what he has to say about happiness, hope and despair. Leopardi's pessimism may be off-putting for many, but for some, it is a refreshingly honest assessment of the human condition. Schopenhauer (1966b) praised Leopardi for his exhaustive exploration of the wretched nature of our existence, finding his approach uplifting rather than depressing: 'He presents it on every page of his works, yet in such a multiplicity of forms and applications, with such a wealth of imagery, that he never wearies us, but, on the contrary, has a diverting and stimulating effect' (p. 588). Unamuno (1972) too, expresses deep admiration for the burden carried by the Italian thinker, depicting him, with others who shared a similarly tragic vision, as someone who was 'weighed down with wisdom rather than with knowledge' (p. 22). Leopardi's rendering of our fate is 'darkly comic' rather than dismissive; unlike Rousseau, whom he read and respected, Leopardi favoured not withdrawal from but engagement with the circumstances in which we find ourselves (Dienstag, 2006, pp. 50, 52). Like Unamuno, Leopardi could see that the origins of our despair lie in our reflective, reasoning consciousness. Unamuno's memorable portrayal of consciousness as a 'disease' (Unamuno, 1972) is mirrored in Leopardi's recognition that knowledge is 'at once enduring and poisonous' (Dienstag, 2006, p. 53). Simone Weil (1997, 2001) was likewise sharply aware of the limits of 'intelligence' and argued for the cultivation of a form of attention that involved a letting go of some of our usual categories for understanding. In Weil, as in Leopardi, there is a willingness to face rather than flee from the realities of existence. In Weil's terms, this means occupying a space she calls 'the void', not with a sense of debilitating fear, but with calmness and equanimity. This attitude applies whether our experiences are joyous or painful. Suffering, Weil – and Leopardi – understood, can 'teach' us, but only if we are willing to put aside some of our usual preconceptions, adopt a more open posture and wait.

As Valiunas (2022) observes, the *Zibaldone* 'records the uncontrollable twitches and grimaces of a man in severe psychic pain, but also his tireless dedication to the life of the mind that takes all learning as its province and is curious even about the daily round of ordinary life, which most intellectuals consider beneath their notice' (p. 28). Leopardi was 'the most honest and most forgiving of humanists' (p. 31). For him, 'the best of men is he who accepts his fate even though he knows his life is meaningless; he fears nothing and tolerates no saving illusion. His satisfaction lies in his contempt for nature and fate, in the philosophic iron in the soul' (p. 31). The problem Leopardi poses is '[h]ow to live without hope of happiness or even relief from misery in this life, or without hope of anything at all after death' (p. 31). Leopardi sees honour in lucidity and in 'the courageous denial of all consolation except that provided by the beauty of the poem he creates' (p. 31). Art does not provide a panacea for life's ills. It does not overcome the unhappiness and despair fundamental to all human existence. But it can provide glimpses of beauty, of something greater than ourselves. Art can play a role – often a vital one – in allowing us to go on, when all seems lost. Valiunas captures Leopardi's position thus: 'Nothingness taken straight up kills the spirit with an arctic blast, but nothingness rendered artfully by a master lifts one out of despondency and heats the blood' (p. 28). Leopardi's allure lies in 'his clarity of vision and unwavering fortitude' (p. 33). As a thinker, a poet and a human being, he does not seek to 'overcome' God, or nature, or himself. In Leopardi's stark portrait of our fate, we find, in the end, an ethic of acceptance. Acceptance for Leopardi does not mean the denial of hope, but hope too must ultimately be accepted as illusory. Leopardi could not find faith in God, and he could not find faith in reason. He did not believe in human progress, and he did not think science would solve the deepest problems that plague us. Acceptance does not provide a means of escape; nor does it grant us relief from our suffering. Acceptance is, however, all that is left for us when we peer as far as we can down the barrel of existence. We may reach a position of acceptance only after having fought our way through the thickets of a lifetime of struggle. If we attain any wisdom in life, we should not expect this to make our existence any easier. Wisdom is hard won, and acceptance 'of sorrow, boredom, failure, and death' is 'the hardest part of wisdom' (p. 33).

Care is needed in discussing how Leopardi's views came to be formed. Leopardi anticipated, and explicitly rejected, the notion that his gloomy appraisal of our condition could be attributed to the suffering he experienced in his own life. For many years, he endured great physical pain, with a deformity of the spine and considerable trouble with his eyes and his nerves. One relatively recent appraisal of his situation has been provided by Sganzerla and Riva (2017), who suggest that 'Leopardi may have been affected by juvenile ankylosing spondylitis, conditioning spinal deformities, relapsing-remitting uveitis, urinary tract and bowel tract problems, and acute arthritis' (p. 223). They continue: 'Chest deformity, as a complication of juvenile ankylosing spondylitis, may have caused progressive cardiorespiratory failure, worsened by recurrent bronchial and pulmonary complications, until his death caused by acute right ventricular heart failure' (p. 223). They argue that these serious challenges had a direct bearing on Leopardi's view of the world, undermining the authority of the ideas he advanced: 'His philosophical theories appear as the result of depressive and melancholic state, related to his precarious health conditions, so limiting their intrinsic values' (p. 223). Leopardi himself was uncompromising in his dismissal of this kind of reasoning. He was clear that any attempt to reduce his philosophical views to nothing more than a manifestation of his personal difficulties would be an act of cowardice. In a letter composed in 1832, Leopardi insisted: 'However great my sufferings may have been, I do not seek to diminish them by comforting myself with vain hopes, and thoughts of a future and unknown happiness' (Edwardes, 1882, p. xxvii). 'This same courage of my convictions', he adds, 'has led me to a philosophy of despair, which I do not hesitate to accept' (pp. xxvii–xxviii). Speaking of despair as a defining feature of human existence is a sign not of weakness but of strength. 'I would', Leopardi concludes, 'beg of my readers to burn my writings rather than attribute them to my sufferings' (p. xxviii). Earlier in his adulthood, in an 1818 letter, he had confessed that he thought he would die 'within two to three years'; he had, he declared, ruined himself with 'seven years of immoderate and incessant study' (p. xii). 'I am conscious', he says, 'that my life cannot be other than unhappy, yet I am not frightened; and if I could in any way be useful, I would endeavour to bear my condition without losing heart' (p. xii). Already, he had passed years 'so full of bitterness, that it seems impossible for worse to succeed them' (pp. xii–xiii). He was, we now know, wrong in this prediction – more testing years were to come – but was, if we are to believe his own account, well prepared for the difficulties awaiting him: 'I will not despair even if my sufferings do increase … I am born for endurance' (p. xiii).

There is in these proclamations something of the spirit of resistance we find in the work of a number of other later writers in the existentialist tradition. Unamuno once more provides an obvious example. In *The Tragic Sense of Life* (Unamuno, 1972), Unamuno contends that our response to the pain we experience should be to rub salt and vinegar into the wound. As we shall see later in this book, Unamuno wanted, desperately, to hold on to life; to be immortal. Nothing was more horrific to him than the idea of an eternal nothingness. To suffer, he would say, is still to live, and continuing to exist as a suffering being is preferable to the prospect of non-existence. In both Leopardi and Unamuno, there is, it might be said, an element of bravado in these claims. Unamuno did not suffer physical difficulties of the kind endured by Leopardi, but he had a tumultuous professional life and, more significantly, he underwent a titanic process of inner struggle. For both thinkers, there is at times almost a sense of pride in their willingness to suffer. And in the case of the Unamuno, there is an educational imperative implied by the desperate need to live on, and to know that one is doing so: our task, if we share this view, is to 'wake up' our fellow human beings. A death that means nothingness is the ultimate form of sleep, and we must constantly remind ourselves – and others – that we are conscious, alive, with thoughts and feelings, hopes and dreams, fears and failings. We must, Unamuno argues, actively create lives of restless longing. Teaching, in Unamuno's hands, becomes a process of rattling cages, of shaking up what might otherwise slowly dissolve and disappear. There is, for Unamuno, nothing easy or relaxing about the process of education; it is, literally, a life-giving endeavour.

We can respect both Leopardi and Unamuno for facing their respective struggles head on and for 'speaking back' to critics, real and imagined, who might be too quick to devalue what they have to say just because they find it too confronting, too unsettling, too 'negative'. At the same time, we must not let either thinker 'off the hook' too easily. Leopardi may not have accepted the view that his ideas were nothing more than an expression of the pain he experienced, but the fact that he went out of his way to formulate a response to such a claim suggests that he at least considered this possibility. Perhaps neither he nor those who assess his intellectual contribution in this way are quite right. A more reasonable explanation is surely that his ideas were *shaped by but not reduceable to* the physical difficulties he experienced. As Paulo Freire would have said, he was *conditioned but not determined* by his circumstances (see Roberts, 2022). Pain was an ever-present reality for Leopardi, and it is hard to imagine that this wouldn't be reflected, to some extent, in what he had to say about life. But this takes nothing away from the perceptiveness of his observations on the human condition more generally. Similarly, his claims about his own ability to endure can be seen as a personal and practical response to a real and pressing set of problems; a survival strategy, if you like. But this need not deter us from finding something of more universal philosophical value in what he has to say. Leopardi demonstrated great fortitude in facing his physical difficulties, and we can learn from his example. We can also pay attention to what the *Zibaldone* has to tell us about the nature of human endurance – about the importance of art and hope, for example, in enabling us to go on – while feeling more than a touch of sadness in the fact that such a brilliant mind did not endure for longer. We can imagine what Leopardi might have said and done in the decades that followed, had he enjoyed a long life, aware that some poets, talented though they may have been in their youth, produce their best work in their maturity.

With Unamuno too, we must consider both the man and the ideas. Indeed, this is what the Spanish thinker himself counselled us to do. In *The Tragic Sense of Life*, Unamuno (1972) speaks of wanting to know Spinoza in this way, and he applies a similar logic in discussing Kierkegaard, Nietzsche and Leopardi. Unamuno longed to believe in God and eternal life as others did, committing themselves to a life of faith, without question, accepting the orthodoxy handed down by the church. But he could not, and for him, there was a continuous struggle between his wants and feelings on the one hand and the voice of critical reason on the other. Unamuno had doubts and was not easily swayed by either promises of everlasting bliss or threats of eternal damnation. He could speak of the torments of hell as if they were no worse than nothingness only because he did not truly believe he was destined for such a future. We can wonder just how far this stance might have been taken, in practice, and ask if there are no circumstances under which Unamuno would wish to escape from it all, disappear forever as a conscious being (see further, Roberts et al., 2023). There are cases of torture so extreme that those subject to such cruelty beg for their demise. In a more moderate sense, most of us are aware of situations where an elderly person simply reaches a point of being, or feeling, 'ready to go'. Death as nothingness can be seen as a form of release, perhaps a liberation of sorts. Unamuno did not see it this way and rebelled against the prospect of his obliteration – the permanent disappearance of his consciousness – with every fibre in his being. It was this very attitude, however, that perhaps obscured his vision somewhat, preventing him from taking other positions on death more seriously.

Leopardi admitted that he had at a certain point in his sufferings contemplated suicide, but he did not go down this path, and had concluded, it might be surmised, that life was still worth living – despite the fact that it brought him little but unhappiness and despair. For Unamuno, the idea of committing suicide would have been terrifying – and at odds with his whole approach to life. The youthful Leopardi may have seen a certain nobility in suffering, but we will never know whether this stance might have been tempered by age and further life experience. Unamuno was granted a much longer life than his Italian predecessor, but he remained a restless soul right up to the moment of his death. To the end, Unamuno wanted to continue not as some idealised or abstracted version of himself but as the imperfect, unique individual he was. What both thinkers have to teach us is that, regardless of how many years we end up having as conscious beings, there is much more to life than we are typically encouraged to see. Leopardi and Unamuno bring a rejuvenating frankness to conversations about the nature of human existence. Their focus on pain and suffering and struggle may seem, in our relentlessly 'positive' age, disarmingly unpalatable. Yet, precisely by revealing more of what we can expect if we exercise our capacity for critical thought, Leopardi and Unamuno also help us to better appreciate the glimpses of light we can detect in the darkness. They show, in their written work and in the way they lived their lives, that hope can still be found – and best understood – in the midst of despair.

Leopardi may paint what seems like a nightmarish portrait of the human condition, but taking such a 'no holds barred' view can also be liberating. This despairing Italian poet can help us to grasp just how important our 'illusions' are in sustaining us, in part by allowing us to see them *as* illusions. We can marvel at the human capacity to go on – to continue existing and to *want* to do so – despite the sobering realities of life. Leopardi takes his cues from nature – from how things work beyond the sphere of human activity – but there is another way we can approach these questions. We can retain a focus on ourselves as human beings but look more closely at our relationships, our connections, with others. It is true that Leopardi speaks of solitude as the preferred state for reflective individuals: 'the wiser and more learned man is, that is, the more he knows and feels the unhappiness of truth, the more he loves the solitude that makes him forget it, or removes it from his sight' (p. 346). In the past, those who suffered misfortune sought out the company of others as a means of fleeing from themselves; now, however, for those who are sensitive and knowledgeable, 'the presence of society is simply the presence of misery, and emptiness' (p. 346). But Leopardi is only partially right here. In solitude, we never completely escape from others, just as we can never flee, fully and finally, from ourselves. The others who, in their various ways, contribute to our social lives, continue to 'inhabit' us, leaving their mark on our thoughts, feelings, decisions and actions, even as we distance ourselves from them. The presence of others may be a reminder of our misery but that is exactly the point: it is *our* misery.

One 'answer' to the question of why we might want to go on, notwithstanding the despair that underpins all human existence, is precisely that *we are not alone*. We can recognise that others suffer too, and this act of recognition can be seen as an educational gesture. More correctly, we might say that our lives can consist of myriad such gestures, repeated, again and again, so long as we keep learning. This requires a certain posture in facing the realities Leopardi portrays so starkly for us. We must, as far as possible, be open, humble, patient, attentive.[13] Honesty and reflectiveness are also necessary in recognising that we are all, in our own ways, fragile, flawed human beings. We can be more forgiving of others, perhaps more tolerant in our dealings with them, if we have the capacity – and the inclination – to examine ourselves in this light. This is not to diminish our differences or to deny the importance of attending to our own needs. We can respect the integrity and uniqueness of the individual while also realising that we are not *just* individuals. We exist as social beings, shaped by our relations with others and the wider world. To more deeply understand ourselves, then, we need to be prepared to look beyond ourselves. This point gains special significance when we consider the potentially terrifying realities of human existence. Leopardi's gift to us lies not just in his exquisite poetry and prose but in the very feature of his work that might at first glance seem most off-putting: his emphasis on despair and unhappiness. What may seem like a debilitatingly pessimistic outlook on life can also be enabling. Leopardi opens the door for a much stronger and deeper sense of solidarity with our fellow human beings – with *others who suffer too*. Life experienced just in individual terms may seem pointless, but when the focus shifts away from ourselves, fresh hope, illusory though it may be, can be generated.

What are the educational implications of starting from a point of recognising that others suffer, as we do? We can answer this question from the standpoint of individual learners, but we can also ask what it might mean for teachers – for those who have a responsibility for others, either in formal institutional settings or informally in families and communities. A prior question needs to be addressed, however, and that has to do with what we understand education to be. Education is, in many contexts, seen as highly desirable – as unquestionably worthwhile. We might problematise certain practices that occur in institutions such as schools but in doing so, will often argue that what is going on those cases is not 'real' education. We may see some approaches to teaching as indoctrination rather than education. If a process or practice is construed as genuinely educational, it will typically be cast in a favourable light. Education is something we are encouraged to want, for ourselves and

---

[13] These ideas find further development in chapter 3, where the work of Simone Weil is examined.

our children. This is reflected in the pronouncements made by politicians and other leaders in times of crisis. Providing education for those denied it through poverty or war, for example, is often seen as a priority. In becoming educated, we expect our lives to be *better*, not worse, than they otherwise would be.[14]

Leopardi prompts us to question these assumptions. If education is, among other things, concerned with the development of reason, we will, Leopardi's work suggests, suffer the consequences of this. Reason heightens our sense of dissatisfaction with ourselves and the world. It takes us further away from nature. Indeed, Leopardi contends, '[t]he utmost extent of reason consists in knowing that whatever it has taught us beyond nature is useless and harmful, and whatever it has taught us that is good we already know from nature' (p. 654). It can diminish the sense of purpose we have in life, allowing us to grasp, with frightening clarity, the pointlessness of our existence. Reason prods and probes and awakens. It prevents us from lulling ourselves to sleep with the process of living. With our faculty of reason developed to the highest degree, we become perpetually uncomfortable and forever unhappy. Reason is, in Leopardi's words, 'poisonous to life' (p. 654). There is only a change for the better here if we accept that swallowing the poison of reason fortifies us in some way, opening our eyes and hardening us up to endure whatever comes our way. But this is a long way from conventional constructions of what is good, what is beneficial for us, in education. There are, moreover, other ways, from a Leopardian point of view, in which education might be seen as not wholly desirable.

If, beyond facilitating the cultivation of our ability to reason, education involves the acquisition of knowledge, this too will, if Leopardi's ideas have any weight, lead us further away from our natural state and more deeply into despair. We carry the knowledge we gain as an enormous burden on our backs. This can be interpreted metaphorically but in Leopardi's case, there was also a literal dimension to the connection between knowledge and spinal difficulties. The countless hours Leopardi devoted to study contributed directly to the deformity in his back, a condition he had to live with throughout his short adult life. Of course, it is not the case that knowledge offers nothing of value. Knowledge can, it must be stressed (and Leopardi's experience confirms this), open up pathways for inquiry that would otherwise be closed. We can learn more about mathematics, literature, geography, history and so on. But we also learn more about ourselves, and not in a manner that makes our lives easier or more pleasurable. Knowledge, like reason, can leave us feeling exhausted, weary with our

---

14 On the idea that education implies a change for the better, see Peters (1970).

existence. Engaging in scholarly activities, with a view to expanding our knowledge in particular subject areas, is, in Leopardi's worldview, not a 'natural' thing to do. We might question Leopardi's account of what is 'natural' and 'unnatural', but the logic of his position on knowledge, when considered in relation to his overall philosophical orientation, is sound: actively seeking to know *more* about something distances us from what we would otherwise accept as given.

In response to the claim that we are naturally curious, and will therefore always seek to know, Leopardi would disagree: 'Curiosity, or the desire to know, is for the most part simply the effect of knowledge' (p. 335). Curiosity, then, does not give rise to knowledge; it emerges from it. Human beings are not 'drawn irresistibly toward truth and knowledge' (p. 335); for much of our history, and for many today, ignorance and imagination have sufficed. Curiosity is a 'corrupt' attribute that has developed further than it should have and changed over time (p. 335). In cultivating our capacity for curiosity, we have made our lives more difficult than they need to be. What we need to know, as Leopardi sees it, is already there, in nature. Creating further complexity in trying to sort and categorise and separate different domains of knowledge can impede our ability to see what is, as it were, right in front of us. We may wish we could be like those who know less, but find ourselves, having gained knowledge, facing the horror of being unable to go back.[15] Once we 'know' something, we cannot 'unknow' it, and this can haunt us for the rest of our lives. This possibility does not mean we should abandon the idea of education altogether, but it does add a note of caution to our efforts as both teachers and learners. If we commit ourselves to learning – if we allow curiosity to lead us down the path of knowledge – we risk making our lives more difficult, more stressful, more distressing, than they might otherwise have been. In teaching, our decisions and actions carry even greater weight, for they bear on the lives of others. We must be prepared, as teachers in a variety of conceivable contexts, for the prospect that what we do could contribute, directly or indirectly, to the suffering students experience.

Much depends here on how we understand suffering and its place in human lives. For Leopardi, as for many other thinkers in the pessimistic tradition, it is not a matter of 'advocating' suffering but of acknowledging it and attempting to understand it. It is our shared experience of suffering, whatever form this may take, that allows us to feel compassion for others. The pain we

---

15 This idea is explored in Kierkegaard's *Philosophical Fragments* (see Kierkegaard, 1985; Roberts, 2022, chapter 2).

experience as individuals, while always distinctively our own in its details, can nonetheless open our minds to the possibility of similar difficulties in others. As Leopardi sees it, 'nothing is more inimical to compassion than seeing intolerance of suffering, malignity of spirit ready to despise the same or a different misfortune or defect in others' (Leopardi, 2014, p. 166). 'Little or no compassion can be expected', he adds, 'by those who have not naturally been given or acquired through misfortune a certain sweetness and gentleness of character' (p. 166). Recognising that others suffer, as we do, can play an important part in our educational formation. We do not need to go 'looking' for suffering; for most of us, it will, sooner or later, come our way. We need, however, to be open to acknowledging painful experiences, and to paying attention to them, if we are to attain anything worthwhile from them. There is, Leopardi suggests, 'no greater enemy to compassion than seeing someone afflicted who has not improved in any way, who has learned nothing from the lessons of misfortune' (p. 166). Misfortune is 'life's greatest teacher' (p. 166).

Being taught in this way can change not only our attitudes towards others but also our responses to suffering as depicted in works of art. Hermann Hesse (1978) recognised this as a defining feature of Dostoevsky's genius, arguing that the time to read this great Russian writer's work is when we are at our lowest ebb, when we are in deep despair. Only then, Hesse realised, could we truly appreciate the profundity of Dostoevsky's understanding of our human condition.[16] Simone Weil (1997, 2001) likewise grasped the need to sometimes undergo a harrowing process of decreation in order to see what had hitherto been obscured from this. Leopardi (2014) makes a similar point, noting that those who experience extreme dejection and disenchantment with life, or who suffer the most bitter misfortune, can find consolation in art. He has in mind specifically those works of art that 'express the most terrible despair' and 'make you feel the inevitable unhappiness of life' (p. 177). Such works can restore us, rekindling, even if only temporarily, an enthusiasm for life that had been lost.[17] Leopardi himself had this impact on a number of other thinkers, most notably Schopenhauer (1966a, 1966b) and Unamuno (1972), not just with his poetry but also with his prose. It was, as has been noted earlier in the chapter, precisely his honest rendering of the despair of the human condition that provided this restorative effect. Art, Leopardi (2014) could see, has the capacity

---

16 Dostoevsky himself was of the view that in order to write well, one had to suffer (see Roberts, 2016).

17 We can, as Camus (1968) observes, only love life if we also despair of it.

to open our minds and revive our hearts, by capturing, powerfully and vividly, both the beauty and the brutality of life (cf. pp. 177–178).[18]

Conclusion

For many educationists, almost everything about Leopardi will seem strange. Beyond his poetry, his work will be unknown to most. For those who do find their way to the *Zibaldone*, initial surprise at the sheer size of this volume of prose reflections may, as reading gets underway, be accompanied by frustration at the apparently disjointed nature of his observations on art, culture, ethics, politics and intellectual life. If these early misgivings can be overcome, a persistent reader may begin to form a more holistic view of the work while nonetheless finding Leopardi's relentlessly 'negative' portrait of the human condition unsettling, perhaps horrifying. In Leopardi, readers encounter a disturbing, complicated, flawed individual, very much of his time and place, but also a writer with something profoundly important to offer others. Seeing what this might be demands something more of us than we are usually prepared to give. We must find a way to go beyond our initial fear or anger or revulsion in the face of such a confronting account of what it means to be human. As will be argued later in this book, strangers can teach us, if only we are sufficiently open, humble and patient to learn from them. The educational significance of Leopardi's work is not immediately apparent but emerges gradually from the 'hodgepodge' of philosophical insights to be found in the *Zibaldone*. It takes considerable time and effort to get to grips with a work of this kind, and time seems, in our busy and demanding contemporary world, to always be in short supply. From Leopardi, we can learn that our formation as educated beings does not make life any easier; to the contrary, it heightens our awareness of unhappiness and despair. But, as Leopardi recognised, in despair there is also hope, and with hope it is possible to continue living, with a sense of meaning and purpose, and in solidarity with others who suffer too.

References

Baker, J. M. (2006). Vacant holidays: The theological remainder in Leopardi, Baudelaire, and Benjamin. *MLN, 121*(5), 1190–1219.

---

18 See further, Baldacchino (2012) and Roberts and Freeman-Moir (2013).

Baldacchino, J. (2012). *Art's way out: Exit pedagogy and the cultural condition*. Sense.
Bouchard, N. (1999). Beckett: Reader of Leopardi, *Italian Culture*, 17(2), 77–89.
Caesar, M. & D'Intino, F. (2014). Introduction. In Leopardi, G. (2014), *Zibaldone* (M. Caesar & F. D'Intino, Eds.) (pp. xiii–lxviii). Farrar, Straus and Giroux.
Camus, A. (1968). *Lyrical and critical essays* (E.C. Kennedy, Trans.). Vintage Books.
Caselli, D. (1996). Beckett's intertextual modalities of appropriation: The case of Leopardi. *Journal of Beckett Studies*, 6(1), 1–24.
Cauchi-Santoro, R. (2015). "Non che la speme, il desiderio è spento": Giacomo Leopardi, Samuel Beckett, and the Quietist tradition. *Italian Culture*, 33(1), 39–54.
Cori, P. (2016). The *Zibaldone* as Leopardi's self-education. *Italica*, 93(1), 77–91.
Dienstag, J. F. (2006). *Pessimism: Philosophy, ethic, spirit*. Princeton University Press.
Edwardes, C. (1882). Biographical sketch. In G. Leopardi, *Essays and dialogues of Giacomo Leopardi* (C. Edwardes, Trans.) (pp. vii–xlii). Trübner.
Ferri, S. (2018). Thinking the future in Giacomo Leopardi's *Zibaldone*. *California Italian Studies*, 8(1), 1–16.
Hesse, H. (1978). *My belief: Essays on life and art* (D. Lindley, Trans., with two essays translated by R. Manheim; T. Ziolkowski, Ed.). Triad/Panther.
Kierkegaard, S. (1985). *Philosophical fragments* (H. V. Hong & E. H. Hong, Trans.). Princeton University Press.
Kierkegaard, S. (1989). *The sickness unto death* (A. Hannay, Trans.). Penguin.
Kierkegaard, S. (2009). *Concluding unscientific postscript* (A. Hannay, Trans.). Cambridge University Press.
Leopardi, G. (1882). *Essays and dialogues of Giacomo Leopardi* (C. Edwardes, Trans.). Trübner.
Leopardi, G. (2014). *Zibaldone* (M. Caesar & F. D'Intino, Eds.). Farrar, Straus and Giroux.
Mirra, A. (2016). Rhetorical strategies in Leopardi's *Zibaldone*. *Italica*, 93(1), 92–104.
Negri, A. (2015). *Flower of the desert: Giacomo Leopardi's poetic ontology*. State University of New York Press.
Negri, A. & Casarino, C. (2008). *In praise of the common: A conversation on philosophy and politics*. University of Minnesota Press.
Nietzsche, F. (1974). *The gay science* (W. Kaufmann, Trans.). Vintage Books.
Nietzsche, F. (1997). *Untimely meditations* (R. J. Hollingdale, Trans., D. Breazeale, Ed.). Cambridge University Press.
Peters, R. S. (1970). *Ethics and education*. Allen and Unwin.
Rosengarten, F. (2012). *Giacomo Leopardi's search for a common life through poetry: A different nobility, a different love*. Fairleigh Dickinson University Press.
Roberts, P. (2016). *Happiness, hope, and despair: Rethinking the role of education*. Peter Lang.
Roberts, P. (2022). *Paulo Freire: Philosophy, pedagogy and practice*. Peter Lang.
Roberts, P. & Freeman-Moir, J. (2013). *Better worlds: Education, art, and utopia*. Lexington Books.
Roberts, P. & Saeverot, H. (2018). *Education and the limits of reason: Reading Dostoevsky, Tolstoy and Nabokov*. Routledge.
Roberts, P., Webster, R. S. & Quay, J. (2023). *Philosophy, death and education*. Peter Lang.

Schopenhauer, A. (1966a). *The world as will and representation*, vol. 1. (E. F. Payne, Trans.). Dover.

Schopenhauer, A. (1966b). *The world as will and representation*, vol. 2 (E. F. Payne, Trans.). Dover.

Sganzerla, E. P. & Riva, M. A. (2017). The disease of the Italian poet Giacomo Leopardi (1798–1837): A case of Juvenile Ankylosing Spondylitis in the 19th century? *Journal of Clinical Rheumatology, 23*(4), 223–225.

Unamuno, M. de (1972). *The tragic sense of life in men and nations* (A. Kerrigan, Trans.). Princeton University Press.

Valiunas, A. (2022). Nihilism for the ironhearted. *First Things*, no. 322, 27–33.

Weil, S. (1997). *Gravity and grace* (A. Wills, Trans.). Bison Books.

Weil, S. (2001). *Waiting for God* (E. Craufurd, Trans.). Perennial Classics.

· 2 ·

'THE CLEAR EYE OF THE WORLD': SCHOPENHAUER ON PURE CONTEMPLATION

In our work as educationists, we typically take the value of knowledge and knowing for granted. We elevate knowledge above ignorance, and we try, through institutions such as schools, to assist young people in their quest to know. No school promotes itself on the basis of impeding the pursuit of knowledge or suppressing the desire to learn. We speak of 'gaining' knowledge, implying that something worthwhile is being acquired. At higher levels in the education system, substantial sums of money are devoted to research, again tacitly acknowledging that this will bring something good into the world. We endeavour to preserve what we know through books, journals, libraries and archives, both in physical form and online. Knowledge keeps expanding, with an ever-increasing range of subject areas for investigation. In many domains of inquiry, particularly within medicine, science and technology, we know more now than ever before. In some respects, however, progress appears to have been painfully slow. For all the knowledge that has been accumulated over the centuries, we seem to be no closer to attaining lasting peace, happiness or satisfaction as human beings. We continue to suffer and struggle, often falling short of what we hope to achieve, on our own and with others. Why might this be so? And why does this matter for educationists?

One thinker who can help in addressing these questions is Arthur Schopenhauer (1788–1860). Schopenhauer is a prime representative of the pessimistic tradition in Western thought (Dienstag, 2006), but he has also been seen as a 'philosopher of compassion' (Cartwright, 2012).[1] With a prose style distinguished by its clarity and elegance, Schopenhauer was in his later years much admired by those associated with the romantic movement in art (Solomon & Higgins, 1996; Vandenabeele, 2012). The list of literary figures influenced by his work is extensive and includes writers such as Melville, Tolstoy, Proust, Hardy, Hesse, Kafka, Beckett and Borges, among others (Bishop, 2012; Cross, 2013). Schopenhauer was well versed in history and the classic works of the ancient Greeks, but he also took an active interest in Eastern teachings and traditions (Abelsen, 1993; Cooper, 2012). His reflections on willing and desire anticipate some of the key tenets of Freudian psychoanalysis. Somewhat surprisingly, Schopenhauer has received little attention from educationists. Indirect engagement with his work is occasionally evident in educational scholarship on Nietzsche and Wittgenstein, both of whom were indebted to him.[2] But studies focused squarely on Schopenhauer himself are comparatively rare.[3] This is unfortunate, for many aspects of this German thinker's philosophy are arguably relevant to educational theory and practice. This chapter focuses principally on the epistemological and aesthetic dimensions of Schopenhauer's thought, but there is also much that could be said from an ontological and ethical point of view in considering the educational significance of his ideas.

In his major philosophical work, *The World as Will and Representation*, Schopenhauer maintains that our continual striving to know is, at the most basic level, an expression not of the intellect but of the will.[4] We pursue knowledge because we lack something, and once acquired, knowledge leaves

---

1 The importance of compassion in Schopenhauer's philosophy is made clear in the second of his two essays in *The Two Fundamental Problems of Ethics*: 'Only insofar as an action has originated in compassion does it have moral worth, and anything proceeding from any other motives has none' (Schopenhauer, 2010, p. 213). See also Came (2012).
2 Nietzsche acknowledged Schopenhauer in his early work, portraying him in one of his *Untimely Meditations* as an 'educator' (Nietzsche, 1997), but later distanced himself from him. For comparative studies of different aspects of their thought, see Cowan (2007); Gemes and Janaway (2012); Ure (2006) and Vandenabeele (2003). For a consideration of Schopenhauer's influence on Wittgenstein, see Engel (1969).
3 Exceptions from the last decade include Callejón (2019); Clifton (2017) and Kakkori and Huttunen (2017).
4 Schopenhauer published two volumes of *The World as Will and Representation* (Schopenhauer, 1966a, 1966b), the second serving as a supplement to the first, with further reflections

us wanting more; we remain unhappy and unfulfilled. We are, Schopenhauer suggests, doomed to keep repeating this process, despite the difficulties it creates for us. Other living creatures suffer, but not in the same ways as us; as reflective, reasoning, inquiring beings, we actively contribute to our own distinctive forms of suffering. This may appear to be a rather grim appraisal of the human condition, but Schopenhauer offers some hope for educationists in the possibilities he signals for aesthetic, ascetic and moral life. He identifies three pathways for transcending, even if only partially and temporarily, the suffering engendered by constant willing: the experience of contemplative absorption, the cultivation of compassion and the path of renunciation. Given space limitations, discussion here will be limited to the first of these possibilities. The first section summarises Schopenhauer's position on willing, knowing and suffering; the second explores his account of contemplation and the sublime; and the third views his work through an educational lens.

Schopenhauer on Willing, Knowing and Suffering

Schopenhauer's metaphysical, ontological and epistemological starting point in *The World as Will and Representation* is the claim: 'The world is my representation'. For Schopenhauer, 'everything that exists for knowledge, and hence for the whole of this world, is only object in relation to the subject' (Schopenhauer, 1966a, p. 3). Representation thus presupposes both a subject and an object (p. 25). The subject knows but is never fully *known*. The body is an object, existing in time and space, and adheres to the same laws as other objects; it is the most immediate object to be known by the subject and provides the starting point for understanding the world. We find a plurality of different bodies, among the myriad other objects to be known. The subject is, however, 'whole and undivided in every representing being' (p. 5). All animals have some understanding of causality, through the movement of their bodies in, for example, seeking food. But they differ greatly in the acuteness of their understanding and in the spheres of knowledge in which they participate (pp. 21–23). Only human beings are capable of abstract reasoning. Schopenhauer is quick to point out, however, that reason simply extends what is already known through intuition,

---

on some key themes and additional commentary on differences between his ideas and those of other thinkers.

perception and concrete experience (pp. 51–53). The practical value of rational knowledge lies in its communicability; it can be retained by one subject and passed on to another (cf. p. 55). We can be perfectly adept at an activity without an abstract knowledge of how we are able to do what we do; indeed, the intrusion of reason can sometimes be a hindrance in performing a task. In playing billiards, for instance, reflection on what one is doing can create uncertainty and confusion, disrupting and dividing the attention of the player (p. 56). If we are to pursue a virtuous way of living, reason is necessary, but reason is not the *source* of virtue. Rather, reason has a subordinate role: 'to preserve resolutions once formed, to provide maxims for withstanding the weakness of the moment, and to give consistency to conduct' (p. 58).

Knowledge is given to the individual knowing subject through the medium of the body, but the body, in addition to being one object among many, is given through the *will*. We will an act through movement of the body, but the action of the body is the objectification of an act of will. The will is knowledge '*a priori* of the body', while the body is knowledge '*a posteriori* of the will' (p. 100). Resolving to do something is not in itself an act of will; only the carrying out of the resolution, through action, translates deliberation or abstract commitment into willing. We can separate willing and acting only in reflection; in practice, they are one (pp. 100–101). What knowledge we have of our will cannot be separated from what we know of our bodies; 'I know my will', Schopenhauer says, 'not as a whole, not as a unity, not completely according to its nature, but only in its individual acts, and hence in time, which is the form of my body's appearing, as it is of every body' (pp. 101–102). The will lies behind every specific instance of willing, acting and knowing as a permanent, universal presence (cf. pp. 103–109). Will itself 'has no ground', yet it is everywhere apparent (p. 107). Will is 'the innermost essence, the kernel, of every particular thing and also of the whole' (p. 110). It is evident in everything that occurs in nature as well as in every form of human conduct. Will should not be subsumed under the concept of force; rather, every force we observe in nature is, for Schopenhauer, the expression of will (p. 111). The same point applies with the involuntary functions of the body that aid, for instance, digestion and circulation: they, as much as actions we take knowingly, are concrete expressions of the will (p. 115). In seeking to understand the will, we examine individual things and events and actions. Yet the will stands behind and beyond plurality and particularity; it reveals itself 'just as completely and just as much in *one* oak as in millions' (p. 128).

Schopenhauer's approach to questions of freedom and necessity builds on his metaphysical account of the will. As the underlying reality behind all phenomena, the will is 'free'. The will is not determined; it simply *is*. Everything in the world of objects, however, is governed by necessity: things could not be anything other than as they are: 'The whole content of nature, … every phenomenon, every event, can always be demonstrated, since it must be possible to find the ground or reason on which it depends as consequent' (pp. 286–287). To the extent that we are part of nature, and have our own distinctive character, we are likewise determined, our actions being called forth as a matter of necessity (p. 287). At a given moment we may appear, in our individual acts, to have freedom of the will, but with subsequent experience and reflection we can come to see the inevitability in what we do (p. 289). The intellect can ponder the motives that underpin our actions, considering them from a range of perspectives, but it cannot determine the will itself; the will is 'wholly inaccessible to it, and … is for it inscrutable and impenetrable' (p. 291). Willing does not arise from knowing ourselves; rather, knowing ourselves is only possible as an expression of the will. Every person is as he or she is through his or her will; knowledge can only add to this by allowing us to learn, through experience, what we are (cf. pp. 292–293). Knowledge changes over time. Over the course of an individual's life, earlier deficiencies may be remedied by improvements in understanding. What we *will*, however, our 'innermost nature', does not change (p. 294). Trying to influence the will from without, through instruction, is futile. We may think the will has erred in the means employed to pursue a particular pathway, but this does not alter the will itself. Different actions are taken, at different times, for different reasons, but whatever changes occur, the will continues to seek its unalterable end (pp. 294–295).

    Schopenhauer recognises that as human beings, we strive to know, yet he warns that 'all striving springs from want or deficiency, from dissatisfaction with one's own state or condition, and is therefore suffering so long as it is not satisfied' (p. 309). Striving, for Schopenhauer, has no ultimate aim. As beings who constantly strive for something, even if we are not always sure what this is, we are condemned to unending suffering. Plants are alive, but they feel no pain; human beings, as creatures of consciousness, as individuals who seek to know, suffer. As Schopenhauer sees it, the greater the distinctness of knowledge – the clearer the consciousness – the greater the suffering experienced (p. 310).[5] The foundation for the constant striving we see everywhere among

---

5   As discussed elsewhere in this book, the link between consciousness and suffering is also fundamental to the work of Miguel de Unamuno (1972). On the connections between Schopenhauer and Unamuno, see Franz (1999) and Gómez (2007).

human beings, and in the wider animal kingdom, lies in the will to live. Yet the suffering engendered by this striving can become so great that death comes to seem desirable.[6] Even if we do not reach such a state of desperation, death in never too far away. For Schopenhauer, all human existence is a form of dying. We truly exist only in the present, but there is a 'continual rushing of the present into the dead past, a constant dying'. 'Every breath we draw', Schopenhauer adds, 'wards off the death that constantly impinges on us'; we exist as beings with death being 'ever-deferred' (p. 311). At a certain point, having finally cast off many of the cares that had hitherto plagued our lives, we may find ourselves facing a new problem: we become a burden to ourselves, so used to the relentless quest to satisfy desires that we are at a loss to know what to do with ourselves. Boredom can set in, and with it, deep despair; every hour becomes simply another one to get through on the way to death (p. 313).[7]

Contemplation and the Sublime

At first glance, Schopenhauer's philosophy seems unrelentingly bleak. Given an all-powerful will, suffering is an inevitable part of the human condition, and we must accept this. '[S]o long as our consciousness is filled by our will', Schopenhauer says, 'so long as we are given up to the throng of desires with its constant hopes and fears, so long as we are the subject of willing, we never obtain lasting happiness or peace' (p. 196).[8] Schopenhauer does, however, offer several avenues for relieving this constant suffering, even if only temporarily. The first is the aesthetic experience of absorbed contemplation; the second is the ethical quality of compassion; and the third is the path of ascetic resignation. While all three possibilities are of interest from an educational perspective, discussion here will be confined to Schopenhauer's account of contemplation. Contemplative pedagogies have been considered at length by educationists over the last two decades. Some of this work has been purely theoretical, but practical initiatives have also been instigated and investigated.

---

6 As Kakkori and Huttunen (2017, p. 2075) put it, 'The will-to-live makes our existence almost a living hell'.

7 The summary of Schopenhauer's philosophy provided in this section has been necessarily brief. For book-length studies of the metaphysical, epistemological and ethical foundations of Schopenhauer's thought, see Janaway (1989); Magee (1983); Marcin (2005) and Singh (2007).

8 See further, Soll (2012).

In a number of countries, mindfulness programmes have been introduced in schools and other educational institutions, and these have been described and evaluated in the literature.[9] The roots of mindfulness as a concept lie in Buddhist thought, but there are wide variations in the extent to which these origins are acknowledged and explored in reflections on school-based initiatives. There is also an extensive body of work on the educational significance of the closely related notion of attention, as understood by thinkers such as Simone Weil and Iris Murdoch.[10] Schopenhauer has seldom been referenced in these studies, and yet, as the analysis below shows, he offers a distinctive standpoint from which to consider the role of contemplation in our educational lives.

In the first volume of *The World as Will and Representation*, Schopenhauer speaks of a state of mind that leaves us, momentarily, free from the dictates of the will. This is a form of experience, prompted by either an external influence or a disposition from within, in which we are able to consider things 'without interest, without subjectivity, purely objectively' (Schopenhauer, 1966a, p. 196). In this state, the focus is not on satisfying wants or desires; rather, our consciousness is entirely given over to the object of our attention. Such experiences are painless and peaceful; they deliver us, however briefly, from the suffering that accompanies constant willing. Schopenhauer refers to this state of mind as 'pure contemplation' (p. 196). In such a state, we forget our individuality and become completely absorbed in the object of contemplation; the knower and the known become one. This is a form of 'will-less knowing' where the knower and the known 'no longer stand in the stream of time and of all other relations'; it is a state that can come about in 'any environment' (p. 197). It may be a response to a work of art or to objects and phenomena in the natural world. A painting or a scene of great beauty in nature can draw us in, snatching us without warning from the restless stream of thoughts generated by the will. Happiness and unhappiness evaporate, social differences disappear, and we enter a state of calmness and tranquillity. In such moments, Schopenhauer says, 'we have stepped into another world, so to speak, where everything that moves our will, and thus violently agitates us, no longer exists' (p. 197).

---

9   For a variety of different perspectives on these initiatives, compare Ergas (2014); Holt and Atkinson (2022); Norton and Griffith (2020); O'Donnell (2015) and Reveley (2015).

10 On Weil, see Caranfa (2010); Catton (2019); Eppert (2004); Lewin (2014); Roberts (2011, 2021, 2022a); Rytzler (2019); Tubbs (2005); Yoda (2017) and Zembylas (2022). On Murdoch, see Delaune (2020); Laverty (2007); Liston (2008); McDonough (2000); Roberts and Freeman-Moir (2013) and Roberts and Saeverot (2018).

For Schopenhauer, there are two aspects to aesthetic contemplation: subjective and objective. The first of these he explains with reference to the sublime, the second with reference to Platonic Ideas. Beauty in the objective sense lies in the realm of Ideas but it can be perceived through sublime subjective experience. An encounter with the beauty of the natural world lends itself most readily to this form of experience. Even those who are most apathetic, seemingly least open to such experiences, can find momentary aesthetic pleasure in the colours, the sights, the smells, the sounds of nature. Nature reaches out to us, inviting contemplation. Nature in her majesty may be threatening and, perceived in this way, may incline the beholder in the direction of willing. Yet, while acknowledging those tendencies, the beholder may nonetheless resist the sense of dread that arises and deliberately engage in an act of quiet contemplation. Through contemplating not just the objects we behold but the Ideas behind them, we elevate ourselves above our individuality, our individual willing. In so doing, we enter a state of exaltation: we have a feeling of the sublime. The difference between a feeling of the beautiful and a feeling of the sublime is that for the former, pure will-less knowing is experienced without struggle, whereas for the latter, it comes only via conscious, sometimes violent, inner effort (pp. 201–202). Continuing conscious effort must be applied if the exultant state we enter through experiencing the sublime is to be maintained. It is not our individual will that prevails in such situations but rather a kind of universal human willing, expressed in objective form through the body. If the object of our contemplation poses real danger for us, the individual will intervenes. We may experience fear or anxiety, and when this happens the peacefulness of contemplation disappears (p. 202).

The feeling of the sublime can be prompted by a range of different encounters and to varying degrees. The origin of such experiences can be found in light, the ultimate source of which is the sun. Light, Schopenhauer says, is 'the largest diamond in the crown of beauty, and has the most decided influence on the knowledge of every beautiful object' (p. 203). Light can make what is already beautiful more so, as we witness when it falls favourably on a magnificent building. In the middle of winter, even where the light of the sun penetrates, its warmth may not be felt or may be felt only mildly. At these times, the interests of the individual will must be overcome, and we make a transition from a feeling of the beautiful to a feeling of the sublime. Under such circumstances, beauty is present to only a limited degree. If we find ourselves in an isolated area, without a cloud in the sky and with no other people or animals, in perfect stillness and silence, we are summoned to a state of contemplative seriousness. Yet, here, too, there is some movement from pure beauty to the sublime. It is the very experience of solitude, with no apparent demands on us, that can remind us of just how busy our everyday lives tend to be. When we encounter nature at her most tempestuous – in violent seas and with a storm raging, for example – quiet contemplation may be the last thing on our minds. Yet it is possible to approach such situations calmly and with a serene acceptance of our own powerlessness in the face of nature's fury. This, Schopenhauer suggests, is 'the full impression of the sublime', brought about by 'the sight of a power beyond all comparison superior to the individual, and threatening him with annihilation' (p. 205).

The impression of the sublime can also be especially intense when we contemplate our apparent insignificance in a universe of unimaginable proportions. When we place ourselves in the vast expanses of space and time, we become almost nothing. We are here for but a fleeting moment, as small specks in one world among the innumerable many. We may be awed by the immensity of it all and feel ourselves to be utterly inconsequential. Similar impressions can be created when we behold the enormity of majestic mountains here on Earth or marvel at structures such as the Egyptian pyramids. We can admire an intricately constructed church dome or feel a certain reverence towards ruins that date back thousands of years. Through experiences of this kind, we vanish, as individuals, when we contemplate what has gone before us or lies beyond us. At the same time, Schopenhauer reminds us, 'there arises the immediate consciousness that all these worlds exist only in our representation, only as modifications of the eternal subject of pure knowing' (p. 205). Thus, even if, for a moment, we forget our individuality, we also find that 'it is the necessary, conditional supporter of all worlds and all periods of time' (p. 205). A single human life may seem insignificant when seen in the light of all that exists, for all eternity; and yet, the presence of an individual knowing subject is vital in giving anything meaning.

More than this, though, we can find, in some individuals, precisely those attributes that contribute to the possibility of sublime experience. Schopenhauer suggests that considerations of the sublime can be extended to the ethical domain and identifies some of the features of what he refers to as 'the sublime character' (p. 206). These include a tendency to treat others with a sense of equanimity, 'in a purely objective way', not allowing any wrongs that may have been done in the past to colour present dealings (p. 206). Such individuals will have the happiness of others in mind and will 'recognize their good qualities without desiring closer association with them'. They will 'perceive the beauty of women without hankering after them' (p. 206). These sublime characters will not be unduly concerned with their own happiness or unhappiness. Their focus will be not so much on the twists and turns of fortune for themselves as on 'the lot of mankind as a whole'; accordingly, they conduct themselves more as knowers than as sufferers (p. 207).[11]

A feeling of the sublime – generated by our encounters with nature, with exemplary others and with the vastness of the universe – may be possible for many, but only to a limited extent. Most of us, Schopenhauer argues, can have only a brief glimpse of the timeless world beyond everyday experience. Many of us fear situations where we will be left alone with nature and with our thoughts. Lacking the capacity for objectivity and driven by relentless willing, we crave company, whether with others or in the pages of a book. We seek things that will be useful in satisfying desires, whether this is via our contact with others, our engagement in certain activities or our acquisition of objects. We become uncomfortable in situations that ask something more of us, as individuals. With others, we can moderate and manage our fears. In solitude, 'even the most beautiful surroundings [can] have … a desolate, dark, strange, and hostile appearance' (p. 198).

Those who are gifted with the genius of seeing and dwelling within the other realm to which Schopenhauer refers are few in number and strangers to many, distinguished from others by their manner and bearing, other-worldly in their approach to life. Genius, Schopenhauer says, is 'the capacity to remain in a state of pure perception'; it is 'the ability to leave entirely out of sight our own interest, our willing, and our aims' (pp. 185–186). Where genius is present, the personality is pushed aside, and the individual becomes a knowing subject who is at one with 'the clear eye of the world' (p. 186). Will-less knowing is an exceptional state of mind, but for the genius there is, as it were, a surplus of knowledge far in excess of that needed to serve a single will. This abundance opens up the capacity in such individuals to apprehend the 'inner nature' of the world; it also creates a certain restlessness, even agitation, in the face of a present that falls short of filling their consciousnesses (p. 186). Those who possess these qualities will long to find others like themselves and must engage in a ceaseless process of searching for new objects to contemplate.

A genius will possess imagination of an exceptional kind and may, given his or her intense focus on life itself, demonstrate a blatant disregard for social

---

11 Further reflections on the nature and role of the sublime in Schopenhauer's philosophy can be found in Neill (2012).

norms and expectations. The glance of a genius is vivid, firm and thoughtful (p. 188). A genius will typically care little for logic, science and reason. Geniuses may appear imprudent and may be subject to explosive emotional outbursts. In conversation, their focus will not be on those who are speaking but on what is being discussed; they will tend to become lost in their own monologues, seemingly oblivious to others around them (p. 190). In our present-day language, we might think of the genius as someone who is 'gifted' but 'socially awkward'. We may look on such individuals with a mixture of curiosity, admiration and irritation. Attempts to 'understand' those who possess these gifts will often prove unsuccessful and may be met with resistance. Sometimes overtures in this direction will be aggressively repelled. In many cases, quiet acceptance of a certain incommensurability in experiences and perceptions of reality will provide the best way forward.

Schopenhauer and Education

While the main focus in the discussion that follows will be on the educational implications of key ideas in *The World as Will and Representation*, it is helpful to begin by briefly examining Schopenhauer's more direct comments on pedagogical matters in his later work. *Parerga and Paralipomena* (Schopenhauer, 1974) comprises a number of short essays, one of which is devoted to education. In that chapter, Schopenhauer draws a distinction between 'natural education' and 'artificial education'. The former is the process of learning through experience, with concepts being formed on the basis of intuitive perception. This kind of education serves as a sound preparation for the rigours of life, enabling us to deal with whatever comes our way. With artificial education, 'the head is crammed full of concepts by being lectured and taught and through reading, before there is yet any extended acquaintance with the world of intuitive perception' (§372). The expectation in artificial education is that subsequent experience will reinforce, through intuitive perception, the concepts that have already been acquired. Schopenhauer is critical of this approach, arguing that it 'produces distorted and biased minds', with young people who flounder when attempting to apply abstractly acquired concepts to the real world of lived experience (§372). Those who are educated in this way will tend to judge and treat people and things in the wrong way; they will enter the world 'partly as simpletons and partly as cranks', behaving 'nervously' at one moment and 'rashly' at the next (§372). Lengthy life experience is then required if there is to be any chance of correcting the misjudgements that have been formed, but this remedy will often be only partially successful. This is why so few scholars possess 'the ordinary common sense that is frequently found among the quite illiterate' (§372). For Schopenhauer, there is a natural order to mental development, and artificial education denies this. Instead of trying to fill young minds with the 'ready-made ideas of others', we should instead be fostering in children the capacity to discern, judge and think for themselves (§372).

As Schopenhauer sees it, maturity can bring insight that will often be lacking in youth. This means that great care must be taken not only in *how* children are taught but also in *what* they are taught. Rather than relying just on books, children should be granted opportunities to become acquainted with 'things and human circumstances', allowing them to develop a 'clear grasp of real life' and to 'draw their concepts directly from the world of reality' (§373). Children should be kept away from 'all theories and doctrines where there may be grave errors' (§374). These dangers are present, for example, in religion and philosophy; they are absent or minimal in mathematics, natural science, languages and history.[12] Schopenhauer observes that the faculty of memory is 'strongest and most tenacious' in the young and that what is learned during these years 'sticks for all time' (§374). We should make the most of this receptiveness but must be judicious in how we do so, encouraging the young to learn 'what is most essential and vital in any branch of knowledge to the exclusion of everything else' (§374). In deciding what should be taught, especially at upper levels, only the 'most capable minds and masters in every branch of learning' should be involved (§374). Schopenhauer envisages an expansive planning process, with a careful selection of content at all stages, from the 'barest primary education' to the 'philosophical faculty' (§374). The aim would be to provide a 'specially-worked-out canon of intellectual education', harnessing the formidable powers of memory in youth to support sound judgement in maturity (§374). The material selected for learning would, Schopenhauer suggests, need to be 'revised every ten years' (§374). As young people move into adulthood, they must be prepared to keep learning difficult lessons as they grapple with the ways of the world. Novels that present an unrealistic portrait of life should be avoided (§376). Across the lifespan, there may be a constant interplay between abstract concepts and intuitive perception, each correcting

---

12 Schopenhauer rejected the optimism he detected in some religious traditions but also saw that Hinduism and Christianity in particular could cultivate a 'proper, more pessimistic, composure towards reality' (Head & Vanden Auweele, 2020, p. 190).

the other; only when the two have 'completely grown together' might we be said to have gained 'maturity of knowledge' (§375).

In these proposals, we see a combination of pedagogical elements that would seldom be put together by contemporary practitioners and scholars. The idea of learning from experience, in a manner that might have been supported by Dewey (1966, 1997), is evident. At the same time, there is, in the push for a detailed plan developed by the best minds, with a deliberate withholding of some material from children, an echo of Plato (1974) in what Schopenhauer has to say. It is worth noting that Schopenhauer was writing before the emergence of mass schooling and at a time when participation in higher education was limited to those from only the most privileged of families. The notion that everyone should have opportunities to enrol in courses, gain qualifications and be taught by educational professionals, at any stage in life, would have seemed odd in Schopenhauer's time. Seen in that light, Schopenhauer's pedagogical and curricular suggestions are ahead of his time. There is nonetheless much in Schopenhauer's work that rubs against the grain of educational thinking in today's world. This is particularly apparent when the implications of his views in *The World as Will and Representation* are considered.

As noted at the start of this chapter, the process of seeking to know is typically seen as highly desirable and we are encouraged to continue expanding our knowledge through the lifespan. We want to know 'more', not 'less', and those who are adept in assisting others in this quest – good teachers, supervisors and mentors – are held in high regard. The deliberate withholding of knowledge will, with some exceptions (e.g. cases where national security is at stake), usually be regarded as unhelpful and unethical. Schools and universities are promoted on the basis that they will open up opportunities for students, allowing them to gain the knowledge they need to pursue their chosen careers. The expectation is that in these institutions knowledge will, to varying degrees and in different ways, be acquired, created and shared. Some of these functions will be emphasised more at some levels in the system than others, but the fundamental importance of knowledge is never in doubt. There may be anti-intellectual tendencies among some groups in wider society, fuelled in part by manipulative politicians who stand to gain from division and distrust, but for the most part those who seek to better themselves through further study and learning will be admired for their efforts. Knowledge is often seen as an essential element in a good life: a key ingredient if we are to find genuine happiness and fulfilment.

Schopenhauer's work casts doubt on these assumptions. It suggests that the quest to know, as an expression of human willing, leads not to greater happiness but to further suffering.[13] In cultivating our desire to know, we set ourselves up for a life of perpetual frustration, never being satisfied with what we have, always wanting more. Knowledge can sharpen our awareness of the futility of our human endeavours; it can lead to a sense of despair that hitherto did not exist for us. Knowledge may free us from some forms of ignorance, but it simultaneously imprisons us in new cages constructed by the faculties of reason and reflection. If Schopenhauer is right, we might wonder whether schools and universities do more harm than good. Why, we might ask, would we want to support institutions that are, in their commitment to advancing knowledge, complicit in the process of making human lives more miserable? We must remember that Schopenhauer is not 'against' knowledge *per se*. As we have seen, he distinguishes between knowing that arises from individual willing and will-less knowing, with various forms of sublime experience that fall between these two states. Perhaps, it could be argued, schools and universities ought to be principally concerned with cultivating the capacity for will-less knowing or at least with enhancing the prospects for sublime experience. It is difficult to imagine, however, exactly what this might involve in practice. The suffering associated with willing is, Schopenhauer makes clear, the *norm* for us as human beings. If Schopenhauer's appraisal of the human condition is accurate, most who enter educational institutions will be doomed to failure; they will struggle to reach the states of mind conducive to sublime experience and will dwell predominantly in the oppressive realm of individually willed knowledge and knowing. This rubs against our democratic dreams for education; against the expressed wish to create systems and structures that allow all to achieve something worthwhile.

For a twenty-first century reader, Schopenhauer's account of human possibilities might seem unacceptably 'elitist'. There is in *The World as Will and Representation* an unapologetic valuing of qualities and experiences available not to the many but to the few only. Schopenhauer portrays the figure of the genius not as an ideal to which we all might aspire; rather, he sees such individuals as necessarily separated from the rest of us. The very act of wanting to be like someone else would itself betray a certain insecurity not evident among those who fall into this category. Our longing to be more than we are ensures that we remain unhappy with ourselves, and our failure to reach the goals we set for ourselves can provide fertile soil for the cultivation of anger

---

13 For a comparative perspective on Schopenhauer's account of knowledge and suffering, see Ali (2007).

and resentment. We cannot, Schopenhauer might say, make ourselves into geniuses, and neither can anyone else do this for us; we either possess the qualities associated with genius, or we do not.[14] And if we have those qualities, we may be able dwell more readily and fully in the realm of pure knowledge – that is, engage more often and for more sustained periods in the process of will-less knowing – but when we are not in such states, we will also experience suffering more acutely. Exceptional clarity of consciousness means '[t]he person in whom genius is found suffers most of all' (Schopenhauer, 1966a, p. 310).

Regardless of the educational arrangements we put in place, we remain, Schopenhauer would say, beings driven by the will, and as such, we will never find lasting contentment or happiness. The expansion of education and the ready availability of knowledge hitherto preserved for a select few could even be seen to exacerbate this problem. Many educationists today might find Schopenhauer's statements on knowledge and unhappiness shocking and upsetting – certainly rather jarring and out of kilter with the expectations we have for ourselves and the students with whom we work. This is in itself revealing. We *want* knowledge to live up to the promises made for it, in part, because we cannot face the alternative Schopenhauer puts in front of us: the idea that suffering is fundamental to human life. In a world where we are constantly told, explicitly or implicitly, that we must strive to be happy and well, seeing the quest for knowledge as a path to despair is a pill too difficult to swallow. When comparing 'optimistic' and 'pessimistic' orientations to life, it is the former that is almost always favoured. We grant special moral status to optimism and rail against anything that smacks of a pessimistic view of the world. We reduce these complex modes of thought to consumer-style preferences, depicting them as simple 'either/or' ('glass half full' or 'glass half empty') choices from which life-changing consequences follow. Allowing suffering and despair to enter the conversation when talking about knowledge and education is a helpful start in enabling us to see what Schopenhauer has to offer.

This might mean, for instance, that teachers be granted greater freedom to talk honestly and openly with students about different forms of inner struggle – not as aberrations requiring counselling, drugs or other forms of therapy to 'fix' or address, but as key elements of human experience. Care must be taken,

---

14 The same principle applies when considering the possibilities for moral development. As Schopenhauer sees it, character is innate, just as genius is. This means that 'one cannot become a saint if that is not one's innate purpose'; one can, however, 'try to feel compassion like a saint feels and stop estimating persons by their worth of dignity' (Kakkori & Huttunen, 2017, p. 2077).

of course, particularly when working with students who may be vulnerable to self-destructive behaviour, but providing a list of contact people or numbers or e-mails as the standard response to any expression of angst or unhappiness is not always helpful. To the contrary, it can be seen as alienating and dehumanising. Permitting students to be 'unwell', in some respects, is a radical move in a world obsessed, at least on a surface level, with creating, restoring and maintaining 'well-being'. 'Well-being' has become a policy buzzword, finding its way into the most unlikely of places (Roberts, 2022b). It has been harnessed by governments, policy agencies, multinational corporations, international organisations and individual entrepreneurs to fuel further capitalist growth and to keep people wanting more. There is a booming 'self-help' industry, with tens of millions of dollars at stake in ensuring that people continue to seek something they supposedly lack and need. We might express concern at the greed and self-interest underpinning some of these developments, but Schopenhauer helps us to see that they are also based on a distorted, illusory view of human possibilities. Education has a role to play in encouraging students to search beneath the surface of claims about 'well-being' and 'happiness', expanding their sense of what might count as acceptable states of mind (Jackson, 2022; Roberts, 2016).

Schopenhauer's approach to the visual world provides another avenue to see ourselves and our expectations of knowledge and education in a fresh light. As Vandenabeele (2011) points out, Schopenhauer is a 'philosopher of the eye'; sight and intuition are important themes in his work, and 'visual metaphors abound in his discourse' (p. 45). Special status is granted to the faculty of sight in *The World as Will and Representation*. Sight, Schopenhauer claims, is not directly connected with the will in the same way that the other senses are. The impressions created by beautiful colours – those observed in stained glass windows or in a sunset, for example – are purer and more immediate than those generated by loud or persistent sounds (see Schopenhauer, 1966b, p. 375). One educational implication of this idea might be that we ought to provide opportunities for learners, especially the young, to come into contact with objects that will stimulate the visual senses. This would be consistent with the remarks Schopenhauer makes about 'natural education' in *Parerga and Paralipomena*. Programmes of outdoor or wilderness education, along with other initiatives built on the principle of learning through experience, might lend themselves well to development of our visual capacities. Through getting out into nature, children (and adults) can better appreciate that which is beyond themselves; they can sharpen their ability to attend, behold and absorb. Learning to look again at the world around us can simultaneously become a means through which we see ourselves in a different light.

There are, however, limits to what can be achieved with such initiatives. Any attempt to 'organise' experiences of this kind will, Schopenhauer might say, already be tainted by the will. We can play a role as teachers in cultivating a love of the arts or an appreciation of nature. We can encourage students to look more closely, more slowly and carefully, at objects or phenomena that may normally be passed over too quickly. We can be 'more visual' – more demonstrative, more focused on attracting the attention of the eye – in our teaching than might traditionally have been the case. But our efforts in this direction can only go so far. We cannot, as teachers, fundamentally change either ourselves or the students with whom we work. We can convey knowledge or play our part in setting up conditions that will enable others to pursue it, but in doing so, we must recognise that in all teachers and learners the will is more powerful than the intellect. As Schopenhauer (1966b) sees it, the will cannot be moulded or improved; its nature is fixed. We can, through teaching, contribute to intellectual development – to what students know and how they know – but the intellect will always be subservient to the will; 'all teaching affects only *knowledge*, and knowledge never determines the will itself' (p. 223). We can, through our educational experiences, become aware of flaws in our character and seek to address them, but no matter how firm we are in our resolve to change, these shortcomings will continue to express themselves. This can lead to frustration, self-loathing and regret. We can find that no matter how admirable a particular course of action may be in theory, the reality will always be different.

Schopenhauer provides several telling examples to illustrate the primacy of willing over knowledge. He observes that among those who are strong-willed – to the point of obstinate, unwavering determination – there can often be a profound lack of knowledge and understanding (p. 225). People can hold fast to their views, no matter how convincing the evidence or reasoning may be to the contrary; in such cases, there is no way to get through the brick wall of willing. The will does not operate rationally, and being more knowledgeable does not provide immunity against the excesses of willing. Schopenhauer points out that our anger in response to a perceived wrong is often quite disproportionate to the offence committed. It is as if an 'evil demon' has been sitting there all along, just waiting for a trigger to be pulled that will release it (p. 225). The will expresses itself in its own manner, even as we look on, as knowing subjects, in horror at what it is doing. The intellect is the will's tool – its servant, not its master. The will pulses with life, full of restless energy. It can never be fully contained, fully controlled. This does not mean we have to fear the influence of the will over our everyday activities. Schopenhauer notes that if a conversation is purely intellectual, it will be 'cold', almost as if the person engaging in the discourse is not there (p. 225). It is only when the will makes itself felt that the person becomes present. The will brings warmth to the interaction, but this can also, at times, take on a form that brings its own problems, as in a conversation that becomes 'overheated'.

In our contemporary world, we might profitably examine those who are steadfastly committed to 'conspiracy theories' in the light of Schopenhauer's ideas. The vaccination campaigns initiated by governments in response to the global Covid-19 pandemic reinvigorated conspiracy narratives, spawning a host of protests, some violent and visible, others simmering away beneath the surface in online forums. Finding a balanced approach in potentially volatile situations is not easy. We may readily concede that in some instances, powerful people *do* conspire, in covering up an unpalatable truth or in seeking to maintain their competitive advantage over others. But admissions of this kind are not sufficient; for those who adhere rigidly to a conspiracy-oriented view of the world, it sometimes seems as if almost everything of any significance must be made to conform to this way of thinking. All major policy decisions and developments, all actions taken by politicians and others in leadership roles, all functions performed by civil servants, will be seen to issue from some larger design, to form part of a giant plan. For an individual wrapped tightly in the embrace of a conspiracy mindset, connecting with others who hold differing points of view can be difficult. Conversations quickly break down, and dialogue often becomes impossible. The conspiracy theorist can argue for a position and even do so in a manner where the conclusions reached follow logically from the premises advanced. But the premises themselves cannot be questioned, and continuing to push in rendering fundamental assumptions problematic can lead to a doubling down on a position, with frequent interruptions and sometimes outbursts of anger. There is a dogmatism at work here that reveals the profound influence of the will over not just the intellect but the whole person. In such cases, we see a marked lack of openness, an inability to seriously consider alternatives. The capacity to truly listen to another person is also missing, as is the humility necessary to admit that one is wrong.

While those trapped within a conspiracy mindset constitute an extreme example of the will asserting its power over knowledge and the intellect, we are all to some degree blind to the influences that have shaped our thinking and understanding. 'That which precedes knowledge as its condition',

Schopenhauer points out, 'cannot be immediately grasped by knowledge, just as the eye cannot see itself' (p. 287). It is not just that we cannot see what we do not know; it is, more fundamentally, the case that we cannot truly 'see' at all through knowing. To put this another way, what we think we grasp of the world through knowledge is only 'the relations that exhibit themselves on the surface of things' (p. 287). Exceptions can be found among those whom Schopenhauer regards as geniuses, but such individuals, as already noted, are exceedingly rare. They may express their genius in a range of different ways – Schopenhauer mentions poetry, painting, sculpture and music as examples – but what all who possess this quality have in common is an excess of intelligence beyond that required to service the will from which it springs (p. 292). Thus, the genius, like the rest of us, still has wants and desires that serve as expressions of the will; what is different in such individuals is their ability to meet those demands while also doing more – *seeing* more, beholding with greater clarity what is really there.

Schopenhauer does keep open the possibility of some wider benefits accruing from the activities of the gifted few. Those who express their genius through art can, in the works they create, provide the means for the rest of us to see into their world, albeit fleetingly. In this sense, we might say, they serve as teachers – but only in an indirect and unpredictable manner. The artist's ability to see directly into the world of Ideas is innate, but the granting of such access to others is not. The artist lends us his or her eyes, but exactly how he or she does this, for whom, when, where and under what circumstances, will vary, for these tendencies are not inborn but acquired (p. 195). This opens up the prospect of bringing an educational perspective to bear on the discussion, for presumably the inclination among geniuses to extend or withhold the granting of glimpses into the world of Ideas might be subject to change, depending on how these rare individuals have been raised – on what they have been taught and what they have learned. Schopenhauer does not explore these lines of inquiry, but they are not ruled out by the logic of his argument. The genius can neither be created nor controlled and will always remain very much a unique individual human being. Even the most idiosyncratic individuals must, however, grow up in a social context, influenced by others, near and far, past and present. Seeing good teachers, as a key component of one's upbringing, can play an important role in shaping expectations of oneself and others, regardless of one's particular interests and abilities.

Schopenhauer identifies a kind of consolation prize for those of us not granted the gift of genius, noting that we can arrive at 'a certain understanding of the world and the inner essence of things', in a 'roundabout way', through 'widely pursued reflection and by the ingenious connexion of outwardly directed objective knowledge with the data of self-consciousness' (p. 288). Our efforts in this direction will, however, only ever produce a 'very limited, entirely indirect, and relative understanding', with 'many problems still unsolved' (p. 288). There is a hint here too of a possible role for education in the practical application of Schopenhauer's ideas. We can foster breadth and depth in reading, reflection and investigation. We can also draw thoughtful connections between the things we observe (inwardly and outwardly). At the same time, we must recognise that the understanding generated by these forms of cognitive activity – these scholarly strategies, we might say – will be necessarily incomplete, always imperfect. That need not be discouraging. Indeed, going beyond Schopenhauer, we might say that grasping those limits, and working with them while also pushing back against them, is one of the principal tasks of a well-lived educational life. Seeing ourselves and our attempts to understand the world as necessarily unfinished speaks to the need for ongoing educational efforts; there will always be more work to do. 'Work' here involves the application of the will – and, with this, the possibility of suffering – but this need not prevent us from acquiring something of enduring value from our endeavours.

Even for the genius, the capacity to see what others cannot may express itself only periodically; it is not in all cases a permanent state. A genius may become deeply immersed in his or her art, seemingly disconnected from the rest of the world, but then suddenly, as it were, fall back to Earth. The genius is, at one moment, dwelling in the eternal and universal realm of Ideas and then, at the next, grounded again in the everyday world of wants and whims and struggle and striving. Schopenhauer is rather vague in describing the periods of time that may be spent in the realm of Ideas but he does indicate that contemplative states can be retained long enough for a genius to 'repeat' what he or she knows – that is, to communicate it to the rest of us – via a work of art. This suggests that for those gifted few, dwelling in the sphere of pure will-less knowing might last days, weeks or even months, maybe with occasional lapses back into the depressing reality inhabited by ordinary mortals. But this is perhaps the wrong way to look it, for in the realm of Ideas, Schopenhauer might say, conventional notions of time are themselves rendered problematic. There is merit, nevertheless, in pausing for a moment to consider what might be possible and to ask whether such states can, through consistent practice, with appropriate guidance, be extended or cultivated with greater regularity. Such considerations are of particular interest for educationists, for they raise the question of whether we can change the nature, duration or frequency of these states of mind through teaching and/or learning.

This presupposes that attaining a state of pure will-less knowing is both possible and desirable. On the question of possibility, we might be persuaded by Schopenhauer but also wish to test his claims empirically. Empirical investigation might take the form of self-reflection and analysis following moments where we find ourselves in states that appear to resemble those Schopenhauer is describing. Or, should we never experience anything like this ourselves, we might interview others who report such episodes or exhibit qualities consistent with them. Undertaking brain scans may provide another avenue for detecting changes in consciousness and, perhaps in combination with the verbal accounts of those undergoing the scanning, provide verification of such experiences. All of this, however, will not take us far enough, for we may also want to ask whether we *ought* to cultivate such states of mind, in ourselves or in others. The relief from suffering that accompanies such states (if we accept Schopenhauer's argument) may appear to provide sufficient justification, but this is not as self-evident as it seems. For, as has been argued elsewhere (Roberts, 2016), suffering can, at times, and in certain ways, be of value for us. In making judgements about these matters, every case is different. The forms of suffering that result from striving to know, for example, can, in some instances, bring educational and social benefits, not just for the individual undergoing this process but also for those with whom he or she works (e.g. students or colleagues). It need not, however, be a case of either/or: acknowledging that suffering can, under some circumstances, ultimately prove worthwhile does not mean we should actively seek it or want to avoid situations where we find temporary relief from it.

There is merit also in examining the process of striving a little more closely. Schopenhauer argues that we suffer because we are never fully or permanently satisfied and always desire more. Striving to know leads to further suffering because what we know, or think we know, is never enough; we always feel a need to know more. But we can come to accept this sense of incompleteness; indeed, we can see it as an essential element of education. Schopenhauer does not seem to seriously consider the notion that not knowing but wanting to know could be a desirable state of mind to cultivate. He implies that those who know little but who are either ignorant of their lack of knowledge or satisfied with this will suffer less than those who keep striving to know more. But this need not always be so. We can not only learn to live with the dissatisfaction we feel in never quite reaching our goals in knowing and knowledge; we can relish this sensation.

Grasping, with a sense of awe and wonder, how much more there is to know – and setting out on a journey we know we will never complete in trying to attain this knowledge – can be exhilarating. It can give us the energy and drive we need to go on, providing us with a sense of purpose and direction. It can do so even as we anticipate the suffering this will bring. We may experience frustration as we struggle with a domain of knowledge with which we are largely unfamiliar. We may be troubled by what we find. We can feel anxious, fearful. We may be filled with doubts – about our own abilities or about the certainty of our knowledge – but still find ourselves seeking to know. We can recognise the influence of the will over this desire and acknowledge its power, pushing on in our pursuit regardless. Education is, as much as anything else, a matter of *movement*, and the restlessness, the agitation, the sense of unfinishedness we experience while seeking to know is all part of this. Recognising that committing to a process of educational development will (in some ways) make us unhappier is not sufficient reason to abandon this commitment.

Conclusion

Schopenhauer's distinctive contribution to philosophy lies in the emphasis he places on the will: on its power and influence over us. The connections Schopenhauer draws between willing, knowing and suffering pose particular challenges for educationists. Knowledge is central to our educational activities. We pursue knowledge through study; we seek to pass it on to others through teaching; and we endeavour to preserve it for future generations. From Schopenhauer's perspective, however, knowledge is subservient to the will, and in striving to know we open ourselves up to the suffering that inevitably accompanies willing. We can gain some relief from this suffering through moments of will-less knowing in contemplative absorption, but, if Schopenhauer is to be believed, for most of us the glimpses we have of the timeless reality behind the demands of everyday willing will be discouragingly brief. The figure of the genius stands as an exception, peering more deeply into other-worldly spaces than other mortals. From the genius, there is perhaps much that we might learn, though Schopenhauer leaves many questions unanswered in considering the extent to which and ways in which this could be so. Schopenhauer, like Leopardi, offers a refreshingly frank portrait of the inner difficulties we can expect to face in life. He helps us to see that suffering is a key element of our existence as reflective beings and that education cannot 'overcome' this. What he does not appear to appreciate is that we can, through education, come to live on better terms with our suffering, including the suffering engendered by our pursuit of knowledge. We can value what we learn, and want to keep learning, with all the frustration and angst this can bring, recognising that our unfinishedness is an important part of what makes us human.

References

Abelsen, P. (1993). Schopenhauer and Buddhism. *Philosophy East and West, 43*(2), 255–278.

Ali, Z. I. (2007). Ai-Ghazālī and Schopenhauer on knowledge and suffering. *Philosophy East and West, 57*(4), 409–419.

Bishop, P. (2012). Schopenhauer's impact on European literature. In B. Vandenabeele (Ed.), *A companion to Schopenhauer* (pp. 333–348). Blackwell.

Caranfa, A. (2010). Contemplative instruction and the gifts of beauty, love, and silence. *Educational Theory, 60*(5), 561–585.

Callejón, E. R. (2019). Utopia and pessimism: "You should not forsake the ship in a storm because you cannot command the winds". *Educational Philosophy and Theory, 51*(3), 335–345.

Came, D. (2012). Schopenhauer on the metaphysics of art and morality. In B. Vandenabeele (Ed.), *A companion to Schopenhauer* (pp. 237–248). Blackwell.

Cartwright, D. E. (2012). Schopenhauer on the value of compassion. In B. Vandenabeele (Ed.), *A companion to Schopenhauer* (pp. 249–265). Blackwell.

Catton, J. (2019). *Attention, literature and education*. PhD thesis: University of Canterbury, New Zealand.

Clifton, W. S. (2017). Schopenhauer and Murdoch on the ethical value of the loss of self in aesthetic experience. *Journal of Aesthetic Education, 51*(4), 5–25.

Cooper, D. E. (2012). Schopenhauer and Indian philosophy. In B. Vandenabeele (Ed.), *A companion to Schopenhauer* (pp. 266–279). Blackwell.

Cowan, R. B. (2007). Nietzsche's attempted escape from Schopenhauer's South Asian sources in The Birth of Tragedy. *German Studies Review, 30*(3), 537–556.

Cross, S. (2013). *Schopenhauer's encounter with Indian thought: Representation and will and their Indian parallels*. University of Hawaii Press.

Delaune, A. (2020). *Attention and early childhood education*. PhD thesis: University of Canterbury, New Zealand.

Dewey, J. (1966). *Democracy and education*. Free Press.

Dewey, J. (1997). *Experience and education*. Touchstone.

Dienstag, J. F. (2006). *Pessimism: Philosophy, ethic, spirit*. Princeton University Press.

Eppert, C. (2004). Altering habits of attention in education: Simone Weil and Emmanual Levinas. In H. A. Alexander (Ed.), *Spirituality and ethics in education: Philosophical, theological and radical perspectives* (pp. 42–53). Sussex Academic Press.

Ergas, O. (2014). Mindfulness in education: At the intersection of science, religion and healing. *Critical Studies in Education, 55*(1), 58–72.

Franz, T. R. (1999). *Amor y pedagogía* and Schopenhauer's *The world as will and representation*. *Revista Hispánica Moderna*, 52(2), 403–410.

Gemes, K. & Janaway, C. (2012). Life-denial versus life-affirmation: Schopenhauer and Nietzsche on pessimism and asceticism. In B. Vandenabeele (Ed.), *A companion to Schopenhauer* (pp. 280–299). Blackwell.

Gómez, M. A. (2007). Unamuno and Schopenhauer: Art, artistic imagination and the relation to modernism. *Confluencia*, 23(1), 43–61.

Head, J. & Vanden Auweele, D. (2020). Schopenhauer on Christ, suffering and the negation of the will. *International Journal of Philosophical Studies*, 28(2), 188–204.

Holt, S. & Atkinson, C. (2022). Exploring the use and delivery of school-based mindfulness programmes for young children. *Educational and child psychology*, 39(3), 70–93.

Jackson, L. (2022). *Beyond virtue: The politics of educating emotions*. Cambridge University Press.

Janaway, C. (1989). *Self and world in Schopenhauer's philosophy*. Oxford University Press.

Kakkori, L. & Huttunen, R. (2017). Schopenhauer and Nietzsche on moral growth. In M. A. Peters (Ed.), *Encyclopedia of educational philosophy and theory*, vol. 3 (pp. 2073–2082). Springer.

Laverty, M. (2007). *Iris Murdoch's ethics: A consideration of her romantic vision*. Continuum.

Lewin, D. (2014). Behold: Silence and attention in education. *Journal of Philosophy of Education*, 48(3), 355–369.

Liston, D. P. (2008). Critical pedagogy and attentive love. *Studies in Philosophy and Education*, 27(5), 387–392.

Magee, B. (1983). *The philosophy of Schopenhauer*. Oxford University Press.

Marcin, R. B. (2005). *In search of Schopenhauer's cat: Arthur Schopenhauer's quantum-mystical theory of justice*. Catholic University of America Press.

McDonough, S. (2000). Iris Murdoch's notion of attention: Seeing the moral life in teaching. *Philosophy of Education 2000* (pp. 217–225). University of Illinois.

Murdoch, I. (1993). *Metaphysics as a guide to morals*. Penguin.

Neill, A. (2012). Schopenhauer on tragedy and the sublime. In B. Vandenabeele (Ed.), *A companion to Schopenhauer* (pp. 206–218). Blackwell.

Nietzsche, F. (1997). *Untimely meditations* (R. J. Hollingdale, Trans., D. Breazeale, Ed.). Cambridge University Press.

Norton, K. R. & Griffith, G. M. (2020). The impact of delivering mindfulness-based programmes in schools: A qualitative study. *Journal of Family and Child Studies*, 29, 2623–2636.

O'Donnell, A. (2015). Contemplative pedagogy and mindfulness: Developing creative attention in an age of distraction. *Journal of Philosophy of Education*, 49(2), 187–202.

Plato (1974). *The Republic* (H. D. P. Lee, Trans.). Penguin.

Reveley, J. (2015). School-based mindfulness training and the economisation of attention: A Stieglerian view. *Educational Philosophy and Theory*, 47(8), 804–821.

Roberts, P. (2011). Attention, asceticism, and grace: Simone Weil and higher education. *Arts and Humanities in Higher Education*, 10(3), 315–328.

Roberts, P. (2016). *Happiness, hope and despair: Rethinking the role of education*. Peter Lang.

Roberts, P. (2021). Education, attention and transformation: Death and decreation in Tolstoy and Weil. *Studies in Philosophy and Education*, 40(6), 595–608.

Roberts, P. (2022a). Truth, attention and higher education. In J. T. Ozolins (Ed.), *Education in an age of lies and fake news: Regaining a love of truth* (pp. 62–76). Routledge.

Roberts, P. (2022b). *Performativity, politics and education: From policy to philosophy*. Brill.

Roberts, P. & Freeman-Moir, J. (2013). *Better worlds: Education, art, and utopia*. Lexington Books.

Roberts, P. & Saeverot, H. (2018). *Education and the limits of reason: Reading Dostoevsky, Tolstoy and Nabokov*. Routledge.

Rytzler, J. (2019). Turning the gaze to the self and away from the self – Foucault and Weil on the matter of education as attention formation. *Ethics and Education*, 14(3), 285–297.

Schopenhauer, A. (1966a). *The world as will and representation*, vol. I (E. F. Payne, Trans.). Dover.

Schopenhauer, A. (1966b). *The world as will and representation*, vol. II (E. F. Payne, Trans.). Dover.

Schopenhauer, A. (1974). *Parerga and paralipomena: Short philosophical essays* (E. F. Payne, Trans.). Clarendon Press.

Schopenhauer, A. (2010). *The two fundamental problems of ethics* (D. E. Cartwright & E. E. Erdmann, Trans.). Oxford University Press.

Singh, R. R. (2007). *Death, contemplation and Schopenhauer*. Taylor & Francis.

Soll, I. (2012). Schopenhauer on the inevitability of unhappiness. In B. Vandenabeele (Ed.), *A companion to Schopenhauer* (pp. 300–313). Blackwell.

Solomon, R. C. & Higgins, K. M. (1996). *A short history of philosophy*. Oxford University Press.

Unamuno, M. de (1972). *The tragic sense of life in men and nations* (A. Kerrigan, Trans.). Princeton University Press.

Ure, M. (2006). The irony of pity: Nietzsche contra Schopenhauer and Rousseau. *Journal of Nietzsche Studies*, 32, 68–91.

Vandenabeele, B. (2003). Schopenhauer, Nietzsche, and the aesthetically sublime. *The Journal of Aesthetic Education*, 37(1), 90–106.

Vandenabeele, B. (2011). Schopenhauer on sense perception and aesthetic cognition. *The Journal of Aesthetic Education*, 45(1), 37–57.

Vandenabeele, B. (2012). Introduction: Arthur Schopenhauer – The man and his work. In B. Vandenabeele (Ed.), *A companion to Schopenhauer* (pp. 1–8). Blackwell.

Weil, S. (1997). *Gravity and grace* (A. Wills, Trans.). Bison Books.

Weil, S. (2001). *Waiting for God* (E. Craufurd, Trans.). Perennial Classics.

Yoda, K. (2017). An approach to Simone Weil's philosophy of education through the notion of reading. *Studies in Philosophy of Education*, 36, 663–682.

· 3 ·

EDUCATION AND THE ETHICS OF ATTENTION: THE WORK OF SIMONE WEIL

The influence of the French thinker, teacher and social activist Simone Weil can be detected in a number of different areas of academic endeavour, including philosophy, theology, political science, classical studies, literary theory, economics and mathematics.[1] There is also a growing body of scholarship on Weil by educationists.[2] This chapter continues this scholarly conversation,

---

1   Of these domains, philosophy (Cameron, 2003; Desmond, 2005; Finch, 2001; Murdoch, 2001; Pirruccello, 1995; Rozelle-Stone, 2009) and theology (Hamilton, 2005; Hermida, 2006; Rozelle-Stone & Stone, 2013; Springstead, 2021; Tracy, 2004; Willox, 2008; Wood, 2007) are particularly well represented. Political and social questions are also addressed in a substantial number of studies (e.g. Blum & Seidler, 2009; Burns, 1993; Meltzer, 2001; Rosen, 1979). Weil's reading of the *Iliad* as a poem of force has been seen as an important contribution to classical studies (Bruce, 2006; Dué, 2007). Literary themes are taken up in Skrimshire (2006) and Vander Weele (2000). An application of Weil's ideas to economics can be found in Heifetz and Minelli (2008). On Weil's relevance for science and mathematics, see Morgan (2005).
2   This body of work has grown significantly since the start of the twenty-first century (see, for example, Caranfa, 2010; Catton, 2019; Delaune, 2019; Eppert, 2004; Lewin, 2014; Liston, 2008; Longa, 2022; Noddings, 2002; O'Donnell, 2015; Roberts, 2011, 2013, 2021, 2022; Rytzler, 2019; Sharp & Gregory, 2009; Torres Olave, 2024; Tubbs, 2005; Yoda, 2017; Zembylas, 2023; Zuurmond, 2023).

with a particular focus on what Weil has to offer inquiry in ethics and education. The first part of the chapter provides an account of Weil's life and work. The second section considers Weil's approach to ethical questions, linking this with her broader ontological, epistemological and political position. Several key philosophical concepts – gravity, decreation and grace – are identified and discussed. The final part of the chapter explores some of the educational implications of Weil's ideas. The significance of Weil's thought for educationists lies in the central role she gives to *attention* and in the distinctive perspective on truth, beauty and love she brings to bear in developing this notion.

Weil's Life and Work

To understand Simone Weil's thought, it is crucial to know something of her life. As Leslie Fielder observes, '[i]n a profound sense, her life is her chief work, and without some notion of her biography, it is impossible to know her total meaning' (Fielder, 2001, p. xiv). This is especially important when interpreting and assessing her contribution to ethics, for in many respects she was the living embodiment of the key ethical principles she espoused. Weil was unusual in the degree to which (and the manner in which) she attempted to forge a consistency between her words, her ideas and her deeds. This, as we shall see, was evident from an early age and persisted as a quality in Weil's character into adulthood. Weil's ethical theory, then, must be gleaned not just from her published writings but also from her actions.

Simone Weil was born in 1909 to a comparatively wealthy Parisian family. Her father, Bernard, was a doctor. In his younger years, he had been an anarchist and later in life he supported the Radical Party. Selma Weil, Simone's mother, had also wished to study medicine. She had been prevented from doing so, however, by her father. Simone's parents differed in their temperaments: her father was 'a gentle, self-effacing man', while her mother was 'assertive, even domineering' (McLellan, 1990, p. 4). Both her mother and her father were of Jewish heritage, but the family was agnostic in matters of faith. Simone's older brother André was an exceptionally bright child, and he was later to become a distinguished mathematician. From an early age Simone developed a strong sense of allegiance to the poor and others facing conditions of hardship. At the age of five, she refused to eat sugar while this was unavailable to soldiers on the front line, and later in her childhood she stopped wearing socks as a gesture of support for workers who had to go without them (Fielder, 2001, p. xvi). As a teenager, she attended meetings of the unemployed (Tubbs, 2005, p. 298). At fourteen, she fell, in her own words, 'into one of those fits of bottomless despair that come with adolescence' (Weil, 2001a, p. 23) and contemplated suicide.[3] She had a sense of inferiority alongside the brilliance of her brother, and this was to last throughout her life. She felt herself to be not only intellectually inadequate but physically unattractive. She eschewed fine clothes and took little care with her appearance.

Having survived the difficult years of her adolescence, in 1928 she entered the *École Normale Supérieure*, where she studied philosophy with Alain (Emile Chartier), graduating in 1931 as a 'brilliant student' (Nevin, 1997, p. vii; Tubbs, 2005, p. 299). As is well known, her place at the top of her class was one above the other famous 'Simone' from the same period: Simone de Beauvoir. The 'two Simones' (Duran, 2000) had, it seems, little contact with each other, but Beauvoir recalls being chastised by Weil for her lack of understanding of the realities of hunger (Dietz, 1999). After obtaining her degree, Weil took up a teaching job at Le Puy. With workers suffering during the years of the depression, Weil joined picket lines, contributed to pick and shovel work with the unemployed and – consistent with her practices earlier in life – refused to eat more than the rations available to those on relief (Fielder, 2001, p. xviii). She gave food and money to the poor and bought books for workers and students, leaving her the barest minimum on which to survive herself. During this period, and throughout much of her life, she was plagued by excruciating and debilitating headaches. As a teacher, she resisted the emphasis on drills, memorisation and examination preparation. She created a family atmosphere in her classes, sometimes taking lessons outside, and encouraging creative thinking. Examination results did not matter to Weil, and those achieved in the classes she taught were 'notoriously awful' (Tubbs, 2005, p. 300). Weil was loved by her students but incurred the wrath of her superintendent of instruction, who was called in to threaten the revocation of her teacher's licence. Weil claimed at the time that this would be the highlight of her career (Fielder, 2001, pp. xviii–xix).

In 1934, Weil left teaching temporarily to work in the Renault automobile plant. Seeking to share more directly in the experiences of her working-class comrades, Weil's suffering was exacerbated by her poor health and she was to last for only nine months before an attack of pleurisy brought her time in the factory to an end (Tubbs, 2005, p. 299; Fielder, 2001, p. xx). In 1936, she went to Spain to support the Loyalists in the Civil War, but her involvement

---

3 Weil continued to suffer periods of despair throughout her life. On her 'dark night of the soul', see Kovitz (1992).

there too was limited – cut short this time by an accident with cooking oil. She was rescued from a field hospital by her parents and taken to Portugal to recuperate from her burns (Fielder, 2001, pp. xx, xxii). Her life at this time was also marked by a number of pivotal spiritual experiences. Weil converted to Christianity but was reluctant to join any church. She had by this time moved to Marseilles with her parents. When the anti-Jewish laws of the Vichy Government prevented her from teaching, she joined Gustave Thibon, a lay theologian, in working in the vineyards with peasants (pp. xxiv–xxv). An even more significant influence on her spiritual thinking in her last years was Father Perrin, a Catholic priest with whom she engaged in lengthy conversations and correspondence. Father Perrin was, in Fielder's words, 'the nearest thing to a confessor she ever had' (pp. ix–x). In 1942, the Weil family moved to New York to escape the Nazi persecution of Jews. Simone travelled from there to London, hoping to join the Free French forces in the resistance against the Nazi occupation. Entry to France was denied her on the grounds of ill health. She contracted tuberculosis and died on 24 August 1943. Her death, it has been concluded, was hastened by her self-imposed regime of eating only as much as the rations provided for her compatriots in occupied France (Tubbs, 2005, p. 299).

Much of the work that now appears under Simone Weil's name was not published until after her death. Weil wrote prolifically, leaving extensive notebooks but relatively few pieces of writing in finished form. Her best-known books are all now available in English translation. Weil was well versed in early classical literature in the Western tradition and addressed a number of topics in Greek thought in her essays and other writings (Weil, 1957). Her reading of the *Iliad* (Weil, 2005) has drawn extensive comment over the years. Some of the lectures Weil gave on philosophy while working as a teacher have been published, based on the notes taken by one her students, Anne Reynaud-Guérithault (Weil, 1978). A two-volume version of her notebooks, translated by Arthur Wills, appeared in 1956 (Weil, 1956). Selections from Weil's notebooks have also been edited and translated by Richard Rees. The Rees volumes include, among others, *First and Last Notebooks* (Weil, 1970) and *On Science, Necessity, and the Love of God* (Weil, 1968), an eclectic collection of essays, originally written for a lay audience, on mathematics, science, religion, literature and morality. Another work, edited by E. O. Springstead, focuses on Weil's late philosophical writings (Weil, 2015). *Gravity and Grace* (Weil, 1997) is an important selection of Weil's aphorisms, compiled and arranged thematically by Gustave Thibon. *Oppression and Liberty* (Weil, 2001b) includes several pieces on political philosophy, with an emphasis on the limits and possibilities in Marxist-Leninist thought. *The Need for Roots* (Weil, 2002) emerged from Weil's period in exile in London, where she was commissioned by the Free French Government to address questions of social renewal. *Waiting for God* (Weil, 2001a) brings together a series of letters and essays, mostly from the later part of Weil's life, with a strong personal and religious flavour. Weil had entrusted this collection of writings to Father Perrin just before her departure for New York. Among these publications, *Gravity and Grace* and *Waiting for God* have perhaps been the most widely influential, but given the breadth of Weil's writing, it is possible to pick out other works that have had greater impact for particular groups of readers, scholars and activists.

Weil's Ethical Theory

As a thinker, Weil defies easy classification. Her ethical position is inseparable from her wider philosophy, and that in turn is intimately connected with the way she lived her life. Weil does not fit neatly into any one philosophical tradition; she is eclectic in the range of sources on which she draws, and she is unique in the way she engages with these bodies of work. Her blending of the 'philosophical' with the 'theological' in her later writings only adds to that distinctiveness. There is, then, no clear line of ethical thought into which Weil's ideas can be placed. That said, it is not too difficult to identify some of the key influences on her work. Plato was among the most significant of these, and the characterisation of Weil as a 'Christian Platonist' (Doering & Springsted, 2004) is probably as close as we can come to describing her philosophical orientation. Certainly, she was much more a Platonist than an Aristotelian, and references to Christ and God are prominent in her later writings. Plato's allegory of the cave resonates with Weil's account of philosophical growth, and the idea of knowledge having divine origins also finds expression in her work.[4] Weil's Christianity is of a mystical rather than church-going kind. She was familiar with the *Bhagavad Gita*, the *Tao Te Ching* and other ancient Eastern works. In *Oppression and Liberty*, she is highly critical of aspects of Marx's work, but she remained indebted to him. Weil is not an ethical or political liberal, but this does not mean some meaningful connections cannot be made between her views and aspects of liberal thought – in, for example, her valuing of the individual human being and

---

4 In the *Republic* (Plato, 1974) and the *Meno* (Plato, 1949), respectively.

her defence of freedom of expression. In her confrontation with the agonies of human existence, she also shares much in common with existentialist thinkers such as Kierkegaard (1989), Dostoevsky (2004), Unamuno (1972), Beauvoir (1948), and Camus (1991). Weil was, moreover, profoundly moved by literature and art, and this had an important bearing on the way she integrated the ethical with the aesthetic in her work.

Methodologically, Weil is also difficult to categorise. Fielder (2001) identifies three key elements in Weil's method of writing: 'extreme statement or paradox; the equilibrium of contradictions; and exposition by myth' (p. xxvii). Weil does not set out to synthesise ideas. Instead, by making claims that at first glance seem outrageous and by juxtaposing phrases apparently in tension with each other, she prompts us to look again – to ponder and question assumptions and ideas we typically take for granted. Like Nietzsche and Wittgenstein, she frequently employs the philosophical device of the aphorism as a way of facilitating this reflective process (see, in particular, Weil, 1997). The highly condensed, suggestive form of the aphorism did not, however, lend itself well to all themes addressed in her work. On questions of politics, for example, she often found that she needed the greater space afforded by the essay form to develop and flesh out a line of argument (see Weil, 2001b). In other areas of her thought – on matters of Christianity, for example – she would often use letters to convey her ideas (see Weil, 2001a, 2003). There is a rhythm and unity to her thought but finding this requires a certain patience. We must seek, she would say, with a sense of purpose and direction, but without an excessive eagerness to attain instant or simple answers.

In seeking to understand Weil's approach to ethics, it is helpful to begin with three key concepts that underpin her work: gravity, decreation and grace. *Gravity*, Weil argues, is our natural human condition; it pulls us downwards in a moral sense, just as we find ourselves drawn inevitably toward the ground by gravity as a force in the physical world. The influence of gravity is evident in our relations with others (where, for example, we turn away from someone in need) and in our moral responses to events we find troubling or difficult. When facing ethical difficulties and dilemmas, it is gravity that leads us down the easier path. Gravity pulls us towards that which is comfortable, less intellectually and emotionally taxing. Gravity simplifies at moments when complexity may be necessary. We are impeded in our ability to resist gravity partly by the sense of self that underpins our everyday activities. Self-centredness and selfishness cloud our judgements of what is possible in the ethical realm. What is needed, Weil maintains, is a process of *decreation* whereby we move away from the egocentric self. We must be willing to destroy the 'I' that distinguishes us as individual human beings, and to do this demands more than intelligence. It requires a posture of humility, the ability to listen and a willingness to wait. We tend to think if we make ethical progress, the resources for this have come from within. Weil suggests otherwise, arguing that the moral energy for decreation comes from outside ourselves. *Grace* provides the only exception to the rule of gravity. It enables us to gain some distance from our own immediate concerns and to respond to the call of the Other. It allows us to enter the 'void' that opens up when a tearing away of some of our usual defences, our prejudices and personal interests, occurs. Grace will often appear only when we are at our most desperate, when all seems lost. Experiencing the void will often involve great suffering – even terror – but it can also bring a sense of calmness and equanimity.[5]

These three concepts suggest a process of individual moral development, but Weil is also concerned with social questions. She advances a view of social justice based on a distinction between rights and obligations. It is common today, as it was in Weil's time, for talk of justice to be based primarily on the language of rights (Willox, 2008). Appeals might be made to rights related to the physical necessities of life (food, water, shelter, etc.), to those built on the principles of liberty, equality and fraternity or to the more specific demands of particular groups. In *The Need for Roots*, Weil (2002) argues that obligations come before rights. 'A right is not effectual by itself', she contends, 'but only in relation to the obligation to which it corresponds'. The effective exercising of a right 'springs not from the individual who possesses it, but from other men who consider themselves as being under a certain obligation towards him'. For Weil, obligations have an eternal importance; a right that goes unrecognised, however, 'is not worth very much' (p. 3). Rights are context-bound; they apply under certain conditions. They can be altered by convention, and different rights will be claimed by different groups at different times. Obligations, by contrast, are permanent and universal. The most immediate and fundamental obligation we have – and this is the foundation for Weil's conception of social justice – is the one we have 'towards every human being for the sole reason that he or she *is* a human being'. We have this obligation 'without any other condition requiring to be fulfilled, and even without any recognition of such obligation on the part of the individual concerned' (p. 5). This obligation co-exists with what Weil refers to as our distinctive 'eternal destiny' as human

---

5   These key concepts are discussed in greater detail in Roberts (2011).

beings (p. 5). It is an obligation to the individual person, not to a collectivity or to an abstract category such as 'humanity'.

For Weil, obligations stem from the needs of the human being. They are in this sense as essential to us as food. We have, Weil argues, 'needs of the soul', just as we have a need to provide sustenance through food for our bodies. In *The Need for Roots*, Weil identifies several such needs: order, liberty, obedience, responsibility, equality, hierarchism, honour, punishment, freedom of opinion, security, risk, private property, collective property and truth (pp. 10–39). Some of the 'needs' noted here might sound odd to the contemporary ear, and some appear to contradict others. We might wonder, indeed, whether they are best conceived as 'needs' at all. They might better be understood as ethical preferences that warrant explanation and justification. Weil does comment in some detail on each of specified needs and she does demonstrate that any apparent contradictions between them can be resolved. She places particular emphasis on the notion of truth. 'The need for truth', Weil maintains, 'is more sacred than any other need' (p. 36). She notes that much of what is encountered in the world, including in books and newspapers, rests on falsehoods. When journalism 'becomes indistinguishable from organized lying', it should, Weil argues, constitute a punishable crime. Weil even suggests that special courts be set up, with 'the highest prestige' and 'composed of judges specially selected and trained', in order to deal with cases of avoidable errors and dishonesty (p. 37). Time in prison and hard labour would not be inappropriate in some cases, Weil believed. Judges would be selected not just on the basis of their training, their gifts of discernment and their intelligence, but also for their love of truth (p. 39).

In addressing the social forms through which her ethical ideals might be realised – and impeded – Weil made it clear that, in her view, both capitalism and Marxist-Leninist communism were problematic. Her critique rests, in part, on the distinction she draws between the individual human being and collectivities. Weil takes from Plato a depiction of the collective as the 'Great Beast' (Weil, 1997, p. 216). In *Oppression and Liberty* (Weil, 2001b), she stresses that it is the individual we must value, arguing for a rethinking of our approach to work and social organisation: 'We want to form whole men by doing away with that specialization which cripples us all. We want to give to manual labour that dignity which belongs to it of right, instead of a mere mechanical training' (p. 18). The division between manual and intellectual labour is degrading and dehumanising. Our principal concern, Weil suggests, should not be with the material conditions of work, but with the workers who engage in that work. Workers must be treated with the dignity and respect that should be accorded all human beings, simply because they are human. The object of social change is not a rewriting of history but a renewal of what is most fundamental to us all as individual persons. Workers should be treated as thinking, feeling and willing human beings, and any form of social change, whether of a 'reformist' or 'revolutionary' kind, will be unjustified if it can only speak of workers as a class or in some other collective way. Revolutionary movements based on the ideas of class consciousness and class struggle can reduce the individual worker to a means directed toward an end. For Weil, the unique individual *is* the end. Weil admired Marx's method – his analysis of the exploitative nature of capitalism – but found his attempts at describing a post-capitalist world unforgivably weak. In Weil's view, Marx's theory was ill-equipped to address the problem of war, and it also did not deal adequately with conflicts within oppressor and oppressed groups (p. 153). Weil was also disturbed by the appeal to science as the basis for distinguishing between different social movements or systems; the idea of 'scientific socialism' was repugnant to her.

The time at which Weil was writing – the 1930s and early 1940s – was one of the most turbulent and troublesome in world history. The previous century had witnessed immense social changes with the industrial revolution and the rapid expansion of the capitalist system. Weil had already lived through the First World War and the Russian revolution during her childhood. The Great Depression, the rise of fascism and the Second World War were to follow in her adulthood. There was, during her last year, a profound sense of unease about the future. It would be easy under such circumstances for individuals to feel all hope was lost. And while Weil had no time for wishful thinking, she also did not abandon hope. Like many other thinkers who faced up most resolutely to the despair of the human condition, she saw hope as all the more important in such situations (Roberts, 2016). Hope gained its meaning, purpose and significance not in times of prosperity, peace and security but exactly during those moments of deepest social concern. Hope for Weil lies in the human capacity for struggle and this is most evident in the most difficult of circumstances. Weil observes: 'The mere fact that we exist, that we conceive and want something different from what exists, constitutes a reason for us hoping' (Weil, 2001b, p. 21). Weil's hope, in political terms, was for the enactment of a principle of 'enlightened goodwill of men acting in an individual capacity'; this for her was the only possible principle of social progress (p. 57).

The Development of Attention: Weil and Education

For Simone Weil, education is, first and foremost, an ethical process. Weil argues that education, whether with children or adults, for others or for oneself, 'consists in creating motives': 'To show what is beneficial, what is obligatory, what is good – that is the task of education' (Weil, 2002, p. 188). Knowledge and competence in one's field of study were important to Weil. As a teacher, she wanted her students to learn effectively and well; in her writings on oppression and liberty, Weil stressed the need for workers to develop as intellectual beings; and in her own education she demonstrated extraordinary breadth and depth in knowledge and understanding. But these features of educational life were not sufficient; the task of education as she saw it had a higher, more 'divine' quality to it. Education invites the enactment of the fundamental principle of respecting and valuing the individual human being, and it can contribute to the process of decreation that is necessary if we are to experience the void and see the truth. Education, conceived in Weil's distinctive manner, works against gravity and allows grace to intervene. The key in opening up these possibilities is our capacity to pay *attention*.[6]

Attention, for Weil, 'consists of suspending our thought, leaving it detached, empty, and ready to be penetrated by the object' (Weil, 2001a, p. 62). In the act of attention, the knowledge we acquire through education and our life experiences sits in reserve, waiting to be called upon as necessary. This knowledge must not, however, make its presence felt too strongly or too quickly. If we are too eager to apply what we think we know we can cloud our ability to see clearly what is right in front of us. We must learn to look, to see, to hear, without being too certain of what we will find. We should focus on the particular without altogether losing sight of the broader canvas on which the object of our investigation appears. We want to attend closely, but not with a kind of closeness that closes – a closeness that makes us lose all sense of perspective. Attention demands of us the humility to recognise that there is much we do not know. Weil considered humility to be perhaps 'the most beautiful of all the virtues' (p. 5). Humility may seem to be the simplest thing in the world,

---

6   For a range of perspectives on Weil's notion of attention, see Cameron (2003); Caranfa (2010); Catton (2019); Eppert (2004); Lewin (2014); Murdoch (2001); Pirruccello (1995); Roberts (2011, 2021); Rozelle-Stone (2009); von der Ruhr (2006); Willox (2008) and Zembylas (2023).

but it is often the most difficult, for our ego, the force of moral gravity, constantly works to undermine it. Good intentions are insufficient here, though they may provide a start. We have to *learn* how to be humble through acts of decreation. Attention also requires a posture of openness. Openness is the partner of humility in clearing the ground for grace to intervene. We must be open to further learning, open to others and open to whatever might follow from decreative acts. Taking the task of attention seriously involves a willingness to accept risks: the risk of having our current understanding of the world overturned, the risk of apparent 'failure' and the risk of suffering and despair.

Attention involves learning how to *wait*. Often, Weil says, we seize upon an idea too hastily and end up being prematurely blocked in our ability to behold the truth. In such situations, we are *too active*, too intent on searching, when what is needed is the patience to allow truths to reveal themselves to us. Paying attention for Weil is not a matter of being entirely inactive; it is, rather, a process of undertaking the actions necessary to allow us to wait. In this sense, Weil's notion of attention bears the trace of Taoist thought. In the *Tao Te Ching*, Lao Tzu (1963) speaks of the sage ruler appearing not to act yet getting everything done. The popular contemporary concept of 'flow' also captures something of the idea that is at work here. When we exist in a state of flow, utterly immersed in our activity, we lose track of time – and of ourselves. When applied in the ethical realm, this idea is consistent with the process of decreation described by Weil. In a state of flow, or in the mode of 'non-action' espoused by Taoists, the doer and the deed become one. Ironically, we might say, achieving this state of integration requires a kind of separation – of the self from some of its usual attachments. We cannot reach this state by dint of effort alone. When asked to pay attention in class, Weil says, students will typically stiffen their muscles, contract their brows and hold their breath and in so doing diminish, not enhance, their ability to pay attention (Weil, 2001a, p. 60). This does not mean that all effort is wasted or that no effort is required. To the contrary, Weil says. Effort of the right kind can bear later fruit, even if it may initially appear as if we have 'failed'. Humble, open, patient, calm attention to the object of study will often yield results later in life that could not be made evident when the initial effort was applied. For this reason, among others, Weil argues that the ultimate object of all school studies (and one might extend this to say *all study*), whatever the subject area, is the development of attention.

In *The Need for Roots*, commenting on the role of teachers in rural areas, Weil suggests that a just approach to education should be based on obligations related to the needs of children (Weil, 2002). The context here is important.

Weil's remarks were recorded against the backdrop of the rising tide of totalitarianism in the early 1940s. A genuinely spiritual way of life, Weil believed, was a buttress against totalitarian forces. 'If children are brought up not to think about God', Weil says, 'they will become Fascist or communist for want of something to which to give themselves' (p. 91). Meeting the obligation to respond to the needs of the child demands a balanced approach to questions of religion, in full awareness of the fact that there is no way to be neutral in these matters:

> The soul of a child, as it reaches out towards understanding, has need of the treasures accumulated by the human species through the centuries. We do injury to a child if we bring it up in a narrow Christianity which prevents it from ever becoming capable of perceiving that there are treasures of the purest gold to be found in non-Christian civilizations. Lay education does an even greater injury to children. It covers up these treasures, and those of Christianity as well. (p. 91)

Older children in particular should be given classes in religious history. Religion is not in itself the goal; what matters is the *beauty* inherent in traditions of religious thought. Weil is against the unreflective imparting of dogma, whether of a religious kind or in any other form. She acknowledges the role it has played in the history of different countries but also points out that it has served as a pretext for cruelty (p. 92). Acquiring an appreciation of that which is beautiful, however, is a universal human need. Beauty, Weil says, 'is something to be eaten; it is a food' (p. 93). Beauty takes us closer to the truth. The response when asked by children who study religious history, 'Is it true?', should be: 'It is so beautiful that it must certainly contain a lot of truth. As for knowing whether it is, or is not, absolutely true, try to become capable of deciding that for yourselves when you grow up' (p. 92). As Weil sees it, religion does not have an exclusive role to play in this form of educational experience. Beauty, and truth, can be found in mathematics, in art and in forms of human interaction and striving. If we are to sharpen our awareness of beauty, regardless of our area of study or work, careful attention to particulars is necessary, for both teachers and learners.

Weil, in Platonic fashion, posits the existence of universal beauty. '[B]eauty alone', she says, 'has a right to our love' (Weil, 2001a, p. 105). Weil advances a view of an 'absent God', arguing that if God were to appear to us, we would be destroyed by light. Beauty is 'the only finality here below' (p. 105). Encountering beauty brings us closer to God: 'In everything which gives us the pure authentic feeling of beauty there is really the presence of God. There is, as it were, an incarnation of God in the world, and it is indicated by beauty. [...] The beautiful is experimental proof that the incarnation is possible' (Weil, 1997, p. 207). This means that for Weil, all truly great art is religious in its essence (p. 207); it partakes in the divine.[7] There is beauty in both nature and that which is humanly created. Beauty invites; it cannot be found or conquered by force. We can desire beauty without wanting to 'eat it' or destroy it (p. 205). Beauty unites the physical with the spiritual. It 'captivates the flesh in order to obtain permission to pass right to the soul' (p. 204). We experience beauty through attention: 'The beautiful is that which we can contemplate. A statue, a picture which we can gaze at for hours' (p. 204). If we are to fix our attention on beauty, the process of waiting to which we referred earlier is essential: 'We have to remain quite still and unite ourselves with that which we desire yet do not approach. [...] Distance is the soul of the beautiful' (p. 206).

Extending these thoughts, we might say that for Weil, all education is aesthetic education. This does not mean merely making the study of literature or painting or sculpture central to the curriculum. Weil, were she to be with us today, would certainly want to give such studies a more prominent place in school curricula than they tend to occupy. She would be horrified by the marginalisation of the arts and humanities in a world driven by an obsession with science, technology, performance, competition and economic advancement.[8] But there is something deeper at stake here. In developing our capacity for attention, which is the principal aim of education at all levels, and regardless of our domain of study, we connect ourselves, through beauty, with the divine. Thus conceived, the process of education is much broader than we usually imagine. Any situation that demands of us the application of attention might be regarded as educative. This can include, and indeed might *above all else* include, those situations where we demonstrate and experience *love*.

Love is pivotal for Weil, and it goes to the heart of the attentive process. Attention can, in some senses, be seen as an epistemological process – a way of knowing – but it is also profoundly moral in nature. It is through love that we bring this principle to life. Weil says: 'We cannot contemplate

---

7   A secular reading of Weil can replace the word 'God' with 'Good' and retain the broader thrust of the argument. Compare Iris Murdoch's application of Weil's ideas in *The Sovereignty of Good* (Murdoch, 2001). See also Delaune (2020); Laverty (2007); Liston (2000); McDonough (2000); Roberts and Freeman-Moir (2013) and Roberts and Saeverot (2018).
8   In a neoliberal world, attention can itself become just another commodity to be packaged and sold to eager consumers. For a helpful discussion of the dangers of attention becoming 'economised', see Reveley (2015).

without a certain love' (2001a, p. 108). Love is an expression of that which we all yearn for: the 'beauty of the world' – universal beauty (p. 109). Love, Weil says, is 'the teacher of gods and men' (1997, p. 171). It is not difficult to see why comparisons have been drawn between Weil and Levinas (Eppert, 2004; Loughead, 2007), for Weil, like Levinas (1969, 1998), places an ethical premium on the way we attend to the Other. Iris Murdoch, one of Weil's chief interpreters, speaks of attention as a 'just and loving gaze directed upon and individual reality' (Murdoch, 2001, p. 33), and this neatly captures the position Weil herself develops in some detail in a *Waiting for God*. Weil suggests: 'Love for our neighbor, being made of creative attention, is analogous to genius' (2001a, p. 92). She continues:

> Creative attention means really giving our attention to what does not exist. Humanity does not exist in the anonymous flesh lying inert by the roadside. The Samaritan who stops and looks gives his attention all the same to this absent humanity, and the actions which follow prove that it is a question of real attention. (p. 92)

Love of our neighbour is, for Weil, identical with justice. Levinas was deeply affected by the Dostoevskian idea that we are responsible to all in our ethical decisions and actions.[9] Weil's position is similar to this. Every particular instance of loving attention toward a fellow human being is at once a commitment to all. And when others suffer, this is our suffering too. Weil puts it this way:

> We have to say like Ivan Karamazov that nothing can make up for a single tear from a single child, and yet to accept all tears and the nameless horrors which are beyond tears. We have to accept these things, not in so far as they bring compensations with them, but in themselves. We have to accept the fact that they exist simply because they do exist. (Weil, 1997, p. 131)

Weil may have wanted to 'accept' suffering, but this did not make it any easier to do so. Her response to those who were afflicted, including people she did not know or who lived thousands of years ago, was visceral and immediate: 'This contact causes me such atrocious pain and so utterly rends my soul that as a result the love of God becomes almost impossible for me for a while' (Weil, 2001, p. 45). Weil's sense of connection with fellow sufferers was unusually acute, but her point was clear. No matter how far away we may be from someone physically, or in time, we are bound to them by the obligations we have

---

9   From *The Brothers Karamazov* (Dostoevsky, 1991).

to every individual human being. When someone is afflicted, what is needed is not sympathy or charity but *attention*. Sympathy can separate; attention connects. Charity keeps us at a distance from affliction; attention demands engagement. Charity collectivises; attention directs us, with love, to an individual human being. Attention calls us to act not because we feel sorry for someone but because, as a fellow individual human sufferer, he or she already has a certain dignity and demands respect.

Suffering can be a teacher but only if we can pay sufficiently careful, loving attention to it. As with all attentive acts, we should not be too eager to learn, too quick to judge, to ready to recoil in horror at what we find. Openness to suffering does not mean setting out to create it; nor does it mean 'excusing' it, let alone 'promoting' it for ourselves or others. Our first duty is to face it; to acknowledge its existence. This is what Weil means by 'accepting' suffering. We should not try to 'explain' suffering, for explanation implies consolation. Any educative value in suffering is not to be found through active searching or in attempts at redress. Suffering should be treated in the same way as joy; both can bring us closer to our destiny as human beings, and often one will be entwined with the other. Weil once said, rather provocatively, that suffering was useful in teaching her that she was 'nothing'. She elaborates:

> I must love being nothing. How horrible it would be if I were something! I must love my nothingness, love being a nothingness. I must love with that part of the soul which is on the other side of the curtain, for the part of the soul which is perceptible to consciousness cannot love nothingness. It has a horror of it. Though it may think it loves nothingness, what it really loves is something other than nothingness. (Weil, 1997, p. 165)

This returns us to the process of decreation. What at first seems strange – an act of self-loathing, perhaps – is, when properly contextualised, utterly beautiful. To love nothingness is not the same as wanting to destroy the physical body, or to extinguish life. In the case of the latter, it is quite the opposite: nothingness as understood here is the gateway to the eternal, to universal beauty and truth.

If Weil's utterances appear at times to be rather perplexing and ambiguous, if they seem to simply invite further questions, this need not be seen as a weakness. The ideas are meant to be troubling, meant to be difficult. From an educational perspective, this is arguably something to be celebrated. For education is not merely a matter of learning that which is already known. As Weil tried to show through her own teaching, it has little to do with tests or examinations or measurements. Weil did everything possible to avoid being reduced to a number, and she did not want the students with whom she worked to be similarly degraded. Education for Weil is a pathway to the *impossible*: to what is unknown and unknowable, but all the more important for that. 'We are beings with the faculty of knowing, willing, and loving', Weil says, 'and as soon as we turn our attention to the objects of knowledge, will, and love we recognize clearly that there is not one which is not *impossible*' (Weil, 1997, p. 149). Our consciousness of this impossibility prompts us to long for something that cannot be grasped. In Weil's terms, this may at times be a source of despair, but it is also, simultaneously, a source of great hope.

Conclusion

This chapter has concentrated on Weil's life, work and philosophy, with few references to contemporary educational institutions. This does not mean Weil's ideas have no relevance to the everyday practices of teaching and learning in today's schools or universities. To the contrary, there is much of practical value that can be gained from careful reflection on her writings and consideration of the pedagogical example she provided through her work as a teacher. Weil attempted, sometimes with comical results, to link 'theory' with 'practice' in espousing and living her ethical principles. If there was an element of theatricality to some of her gestures, this might be explained, at least in part, by her relative youth. It is fascinating to imagine what she might have achieved as a philosopher had she lived into old age. Weil was perhaps sometimes too firm in her convictions, but there was no doubting her sincerity. She could not fully escape the clutches of her ego, and there was at times a mixture of humility and self-centredness in her statements and actions (du Plessix Gray, 2001). But whatever her failings, she left a legacy worthy of further attention.

That word, 'attention', is likely to remain an important part of any future inquiries. For there has arguably never been an age in greater need of a renewal of attention. We live in a world full of distractions, where students often find it difficult to concentrate on any one activity for more than a few minutes. We are, it seems, always 'multi-tasking', usually with several electronic devices near to hand. Taking Weil's notion of attention seriously helps teachers and learners to slow down, to listen and to wait. Paying loving attention to what is nearest to us, as well as to ideas that have been passed down through millennia, brings a breath of fresh air to classrooms that might otherwise be rancid with the relentless demands of competition, bureaucracy and constant measurement. Weil helps learners to live with uncertainty and the unknown. Indeed, that is perhaps where her greatest contribution lies: she gives us a taste for that which is never quite within reach and in doing so connects us with something much bigger, much more important, than ourselves.

References

Andic, M. (2004). Freedom. In E. Jane Doering & E. O. Springsted (Eds.), *The Christian Platonism of Simone Weil* (pp. 159–179). University of Notre Dame Press.

Beauvoir, S. de (1948). *The ethics of ambiguity* (B. Frechtman, Trans.). Citadel Press.

Blum, L. A. & Seidler, E. J. (2009). *A truer liberty: Simone Weil and Marxism*. Routledge.

Bruce, C. (2006). Reading the *Iliad* in the light of eternity. *Modern Age*, Winter, 48–58.

Burns, S. (1993). Justice and impersonality: Simone Weil on rights and obligations. *Laval théologique et philosophique*, 49(4), 477–486.

Cameron, S. (2003). The practice of attention: Simone Weil's performance of impersonality. *Critical Inquiry*, 29, 216–252.

Camus, A. (1991). *The myth of Sisyphus and other essays* (J. O'Brien, Trans.). Vintage International.

Caranfa, A. (2010). Contemplative instruction and the gifts of beauty, love, and silence. *Educational Theory*, 60(5), 561–585.

Catton, J. (2019). *Attention, literature and education*. PhD thesis, University of Canterbury, New Zealand.

Delaune, A. (2019). Attention, individualism, and humility: Using the theories of Simone Weil to disrupt neoliberal discourses in early childhood education. *International Critical Childhood Policy Studies*, 7(1), 41–52.

Delaune, A. (2020). *Attention and early childhood education*. PhD thesis, University of Canterbury, New Zealand.

Desmond, J. F. (2005). Flannery O'Connor and Simone Weil: A question of sympathy. *Logos*, 8(1), 102–116.

Dietz, M. G. (1999). Review of *Simone Weil: The way of justice as compassion*. *American Political Science Review*, 93(3), 697–698.

Doering, E. Jane & Springsted, E. O. (Eds.). (2004). *The Christian Platonism of Simone Weil*. University of Notre Dame Press.

Dostoevsky, F. (1991). *The brothers Karamazov* (R. Pevear & L. Volokhonsky, Trans.). Vintage.

Dostoevsky, F. (2004). *Notes from underground* (R. Pevear & L. Volokhonsky, Trans.). Everyman's Library.

Dué, C. (2007). Learning lessons from the Trojan War: Briseis and the theme of force. *College Literature*, 34(2), 229–262.

du Plessix Gray, F. (2001). Loving and hating Simone Weil. *The American Scholar, 70*(3), 5–11.
Duran, J. (2000). The two Simones. *Ratio, 13*(3), 201–212.
Eppert, C. (2004). Altering habits of attention in education: Simone Weil and Emmanual Levinas. In H. A. Alexander (Ed.), *Spirituality and ethics in education: Philosophical, theological and radical perspectives* (pp. 42–53). Sussex Academic Press.
Fielder, L. (2001). Introduction. In S. Weil, *Waiting for God* (pp. vii–xxxiv). Perennial Classics.
Finch, H. L. (2001). *Simone Weil and the intellect of grace* (M. Andic, Ed.). Continuum.
Hamilton, C. (2005). Simone Weil's "Human Personality": Between the personal and the impersonal. *Harvard Theological Review, 98*(2), 187–207.
Heifetz, A. & Minelli, E. (2008). An economic theorists' reading of Simone Weil. *Economics and Philosophy, 24*, 191–204.
Hermida, J. R. B. (2006). Simone Weil: A sense of God, *Logos, 9*(1), 127–144.
Kierkegaard, S. (1989). *The sickness unto death* (A. Hannay, Trans.). Penguin.
Kovitz, S. (1992). Simone Weil's dark night of the soul. *The Midwest Quarterly, 33*(3), 261–275.
Lao Tzu (1963). *Tao Te Ching* (D. C. Lau, Trans.). Penguin.
Laverty, M. (2007). *Iris Murdoch's ethics: A consideration of her romantic vision*. Continuum.
Levinas, E. (1969). *Totality and infinity* (A. Lingis, Trans.). Duquesne University Press.
Levinas, E. (1998). *Otherwise than being or beyond essence* (A. Lingis, Trans.). Duquesne University Press.
Lewin, D. (2014). Behold: Silence and attention in education. *Journal of Philosophy of Education, 48*(3), 355–369.
Liston, D. P. (2000). Love and despair in teaching. *Educational Theory, 50*(1), 81–102.
Liston, D. P. (2008). Critical pedagogy and attentive love. *Studies in Philosophy and Education, 27*(5), 387–392.
Longa, R. (2022). Reading as *askēsis*. *Educational Theory, 72*(1), 31–46.
Loughead, T. (2007). Two slices from the same loaf? Weil and Levinas on the demand of social justice. *Ethical Perspectives, 14*(2), 117–138.
McDonough, S. (2000). Iris Murdoch's notion of attention: Seeing the moral life in teaching. *Philosophy of Education 2000* (pp. 217–225). Philosophy of Education Society.
McLellan, D. (1990). *Utopian pessimist: The life and thought of Simone Weil*. Poseidon Press.
Meltzer, F. (2001). The hands of Simone Weil. *Critical Inquiry, 27*(4), 611–628.
Morgan, V. G. (2005). *Weaving the world: Simone Weil on science, mathematics, and love*. University of Notre Dame Press.
Murdoch, I. (2001). *The sovereignty of good*. Routledge.
Nevin, T. R. (1997). Introduction to the Bison Books edition. In S. Weil, *Gravity and Grace* (pp. vii–xii). Bison Books.
Noddings, N. (2002). *Starting at home: caring and social policy*. California University Press.
O'Donnell, A. (2015). Contemplative pedagogy and mindfulness: Developing creative attention in an age of distraction. *Journal of Philosophy of Education, 49*(2), 187–202.
Pirruccello, A. (1995). Interpreting Simone Weil: Presence and absence in attention. *Philosophy East & West, 45*(1), 61–72.
Plato (1949). The Meno. (F. Sydenham, Trans.). In Plato, *Five Dialogues* (82–132). Everyman's Library.
Plato (1974). *The Republic* (2nd ed.) (H. D. P. Lee, Trans.). Penguin.

Reveley, J. (2015). School-based mindfulness training and the economisation of attention: A Stieglerian view. *Educational Philosophy and Theory, 47*(8), 804–821.
Roberts, P. (2011). Attention, asceticism and grace: Simone Weil and higher education. *Arts and Humanities in Higher Education, 10*(3), 315–328.
Roberts, P. (2013). Simone Weil: Education, spirituality and political commitment. In J. Kirylo (Ed.), *A critical pedagogy of resistance: 34 pedagogues we need to know* (pp. 129–132). Sense Publishers.
Roberts, P. (2016). *Happiness, hope, and despair: Rethinking the role of education.* Peter Lang.
Roberts, P. (2021). Education, attention and transformation: Death and decreation in Tolstoy and Weil. *Studies in Philosophy and Education, 40*(6), 595–608.
Roberts, P. (2022). Truth, attention and higher education. In J. Ozolins (Ed.), *Education in an age of lies and fake news: Regaining a love of truth* (pp. 62–76). Routledge.
Roberts, P. & Freeman-Moir, J. (2013). *Better worlds: Education, art, and utopia.* Lexington Books.
Roberts, P. & Saeverot, H. (2018). *Education and the limits of reason: Reading Dostoevsky, Tolstoy and Nabokov.* Routledge.
Rosen, F. (1979). Marxism, mysticism, and liberty: The influence of Simone Weil on Albert Camus. *Political Theory, 7*(3), 301–319.
Rozelle-Stone, A. R. (2009). *Le déracinement* of attention: Simone Weil on the institutionalization of distractedness. *Philosophy Today*, Spring, 100–108.
Rozelle-Stone, A. R. & Stone, L. (2013). *Simone Weil and theology.* Bloomsbury.
Rytzler, J. (2019). Turning the gaze to the self and away from the self – Foucault and Weil on the matter of education as attention formation. *Ethics and Education, 14*(3), 285–297.
Sharp, A. & Gregory, M. (2009). Towards a feminist philosophy of education. *Thinking: The Journal of Philosophy for Children, 19*(2–3), 87–96.
Skrimshire, S. (2006). A political theology of the absurd? Albert Camus and Simone Weil on social transformation. *Literature and Theology, 20*(3), 286–300.
Springstead, E. O. (2021). *Simone Weil for the twenty-first century.* University of Notre Dame Press.
Torres Olave, B. (2024). Trains: Attention, and an ethics of the Other. *Review of Education, Pedagogy, and Cultural Studies, 46*.
Tracy, S. (2004). Simone Weil: The impossible. In E. Jane Doering & E. O. Springsted (Eds.), *The Christian Platonism of Simone Weil* (pp. 229–241). University of Notre Dame Press.
Tubbs, N. (2005). Simone Weil (1909–1943). *Journal of Philosophy of Education, 39*(2), 298–307.
Unamuno, M. de (1972). *The tragic sense of life in men and nations* (A. Kerrigan, Trans.). Princeton University Press.
Vander Weele, M. (2000). Simone Weil and George Herbert on vocations of writing and reading. *Religion and Literature, 32*(3), 69–102.
von der Ruhr, M. (2006). *Simone Weil: An apprenticeship in attention.* Continuum.
Weil, S. (1956). *The notebooks of Simone Weil*, 2 vols. (A. Wills, Trans.). Routledge and Kegan Paul.
Weil, S. (1957). *Intimations of Christianity among the ancient Greeks* (E. C. Geissbuhler, Trans.). Routledge and Kegan Paul.

Weil, S. (1968). *On science, necessity, and the love of God* (R. Rees, Trans.). Oxford University Press.
Weil, S. (1970). *First and last notebooks* (R. Rees, Trans.). Oxford University Press.
Weil, S. (1978). *Lectures on philosophy* (H. Price, Trans.). Cambridge University Press.
Weil, S. (1990). On human personality. In D. McLellan, *Utopian pessimist: The life and thought of Simone Weil* (pp. 273–288). Poseidon Press.
Weil, S. (1997). *Gravity and grace* (A. Wills, Trans.). Bison Books.
Weil, S. (2001a). *Waiting for God* (E. Craufurd, Trans.). Perennial Classics.
Weil, S. (2001b). *Oppression and liberty* (A. Wills & J. Petrie, Trans.). Routledge Classics.
Weil, S. (2002). *The need for roots* (A. Wills, Trans.). Routledge Classics.
Weil, S. (2003). *Letter to a priest*. Penguin.
Weil, S. (2005). The *Iliad*, or the poem of force. In S. Weil & R. Bespaloff, *War and the Iliad* (M. McCarthy, Trans.). New York Review of Books.
Weil, S. (2015). *Simone Weil: Late philosophical writings* (E. O. Springsted, Ed.). University of Notre Dame Press.
Willox, A. C. (2008). The cross, the flesh, and the absent God: Finding justice through love and affliction in Simone Weil's writings. *The Journal of Religion*, 88(1), 53–74.
Wood, R. C. (2007). "God may strike you thisaway": Flannery O'Connor and Simone Weil on affliction and joy. *Renascence*, 59(3), 181–195.
Yoda, K. (2017). An approach to Simone Weil's philosophy of education through the notion of reading. *Studies in Philosophy of Education*, 36, 663–682.
Zembylas, M. (2023). The resilience of racism and affective numbness: Cultivating an aesthetics of attention in education. *Critical Studies in Education*, 64(5), 411–427.
Zuurmond, A. (2023). Thoughtful labor: Simone Weil on vocational education. *Labyrinth*, 25(1), 228–247.

· 4 ·

THE STRANGER AS TEACHER: MAXINE GREENE, MADNESS AND THE MYSTERY OF EDUCATION

One of the most important twentieth century contributions to what might be called a 'Continental' approach to philosophy of education is Maxine Greene's *Teacher as Stranger*. In that ground-breaking work, Greene (1973) draws on a range of existentialist sources, both literary and philosophical, in demonstrating that the teacher is a figure who defies easy categorisation – who remains, in some respects, unknown to us. As John Baldacchino (2017) puts it, for Greene, the teacher is 'intentionally kept away from benign or easy familiarity'; the 'teacher-as-stranger plays various roles and typically wears different masks, just as Kierkegaard did' (p. 25). Greene herself was something of a stranger in the professional environments she inhabited; her 'position within an education school was never an easy or comfortable one' and her distinctive blending of different genres of inquiry 'irked many philosophers as much as it irritated literary critics, art theorists and educationalists alike' (p. 25).[1] By rendering

---

[1] Greene's seamless integration of the arts, philosophy and education is evident not only in *Teacher as Stranger* (Greene, 1973) but also in *Landscapes of Learning* (Greene, 2018) and *Releasing the Imagination* (Greene, 1995). For a range of perspectives on Greene's work, see William Pinar's (1998) edited collection, *The Passionate Mind of Maxine Greene*.

traditional constructions of the teacher problematic, Maxine Greene, as a 'stranger', taught us.

This reversal in the ordering of terms – from 'teacher as stranger' to 'stranger as teacher' – provides the starting point for this chapter. There is much that can be learned, it will be argued, from those who present themselves to us as strangers. This presentation may be in a variety of lived contexts, or it may be via novels, plays, short stories or other works of the imagination. The chapter takes Cervantes' Don Quixote as an example and reflects on what this strange character – an archetype of madness – has to teach us. The pedagogical reading of *Don Quixote* (Cervantes, 2005) offered here will be informed by insights from Miguel de Unamuno (1972), Franz Kafka (2012) and Joshua Dienstag (2006). The chapter is divided into three main parts. The first section introduces the idea of the 'stranger as teacher', prefacing this with a brief account of Greene's notion of the teacher as stranger. This is followed by a discussion of *Don Quixote*, with a focus not just on Cervantes' title character but also Don Quixote's faithful companion, Sancho Panza. The final part explores some of the implications of the 'stranger as teacher' point of view for teaching and learning in classroom contexts.

From the Teacher as Stranger to the Stranger as Teacher

Maxine Greene (1973) begins the final chapter of *Teacher as Stranger* with these evocative words: 'To take a stranger's vantage point on everyday reality is to look inquiringly and wonderingly on the world in which one lives'; it is, she says, 'like returning home from a long stay in some other place' (p. 267). In coming home after a period away, Greene observes, we may notice things that hadn't stood out to us before. Some adjustments may be required in relearning customs and rituals. We can feel 'quite separate from the person who is wholly at home in his ingroup and takes the familiar world for granted' (p. 268). What seemed clear in the past may now no longer make sense to us. Cultural patterns that were once well-trodden paths for us need to be made meaningful again by reinterpreting and reordering what we see in the light of our altered experience; a process of conscious inquiry is needed (p. 268). Greene continues: 'When thinking-as-usual becomes untenable for anyone, the individual is bound to experience a crisis of consciousness. The formerly unquestioned has become questionable; the submerged has become visible' (p. 268). Teachers who take such ideas seriously will, Greene argues, 'struggle against unthinking submergence in the social reality that prevails' (p. 269). Recognising that a teacher is not *just* a teacher but also a human being – someone who exists in multiple realities, and not just in the classroom – is crucial. A teacher should not have to consent uncritically to the views others hold of what a teacher should be. Teachers should, Greene contends, retain their freedom 'to see, to understand, and to signify' for themselves (p. 270). After all, Greene points out, if a teacher is 'immersed and impermeable', he or she 'can hardly stir others to define themselves as individuals' (p. 270). Being prepared to act as if one is a home-comer to consider fresh perspectives on what has hitherto been 'habitually considered real' allows teaching to become 'the project of a person vitally open to his students and the world' (p. 270).[2]

Greene's analysis helps us to rethink what it means to be a teacher, and to teach. Being a teacher, Greene shows, is an unsettling, almost disorienting process. In teaching, we are constantly seeing the world in a fresh light and making it anew. It is not that everything we encounter is unfamiliar to us; were that to be the case, we would not be able to make sense of anything. We can relate to aspects of a given educational situation – indeed, often to much of what appears to be 'going on' – and we will have a reservoir of knowledge and skills from which we can draw in making pedagogical decisions. But every moment in an educative encounter is unique, even if only in subtly differentiated ways. Greene highlights the sense of feeling slighted disconnected when we enter an educational environment. There is sufficient familiarity to respond to what we see and hear but we have to keep grappling with the challenges thrown up for us in a given pedagogical situation. If we are to exist in this way as teachers, a certain readiness is needed, but not of the kind we might ordinarily think is required in teaching. We can prepare course materials and acquire pedagogical skills and try to get to know the students with whom we work. We can, and should, have a sound understanding of our subject areas. But readiness of another kind is also needed. We must be prepared for surprises; for what cannot be planned or predicted. We must be open to what comes, even if this may often be uncomfortable. This will mean learning, as a teacher and as a human being who exists beyond the classroom, to live with uncertainties. It will mean giving up some of the control we may seek, but not in a fashion that amounts

---

2 See also Greene's discussion of 'wide-awakeness', a notion she takes from Alfred Schutz, in *Landscapes of Learning* (Greene, 2018).

to a relinquishing of responsibility. To teach is still to commit, even if we can never be sure of exactly where that commitment will take us.

What happens if we shift our focus from the teacher as stranger to the stranger as teacher? Many of the same qualities of educational experience identified above remain but the vantage point differs. The sense of being somewhat thrown out of kilter, of being unsettled and uncertain, is still there, but these experiences emerge from the standpoint of a student – who may, it must be noted, also be a teacher. The notion of being a 'student', as developed here, is not confined to those who attend formal educational institutions; it is a role that can be taken up in myriad informal settings, in a variety of different ways, throughout the lifespan. A student is someone who is open to learning – from other people, from events and situations, from experiences and activities – at any time. A teacher may be a stranger to others, and those others may learn from him or her. But a teacher may also *be taught* by the strangers he or she encounters. To be a good teacher, as conceptualised here, is also to be a good student – ever willing to learn, always open to the surprises that await us as we undertake our daily activities, both within and beyond the classroom. In our encounters with strangers, we may find ourselves challenged by what the mysterious other brings to us or, more correctly, enables us to see. We ask new questions of ourselves, precisely because we have encountered something other than ourselves. This need not be a living, flesh and blood, human other; it could be a character from a work of fiction – for example, Fosca in Simone de Beauvoir's (1992) *All Men Are Mortal* or Meursault in Albert Camus' (1989) *The Stranger*. The stranger could also be an actor in a film or a mythical figure from a legend passed down through generations. Such an encounter need not be immediate or direct; a stranger can teach from another time, another place, perhaps even from another world. It is the experience of strangeness, and the potential educative value of this, that is significant.[3]

The stranger has something unusual to bring to us; something 'foreign' but not entirely unfamiliar. This is an encounter with 'difference' but that is insufficient to capture fully the nature of such an experience. Strangers do not just come to us from without; they can be present within (Roberts, 2013). We can be haunted by a presence that is internal, and peculiar to us, whether we think of this as the voice of our unconscious, or the prompting of our conscience, or the person we once were (e.g. in childhood). The

---

[3] For a collection of essays on strangers and strangeness in literature and education, see Roberts (2015).

stranger as teacher is 'there' for us yet also separated from us. A stranger can be simultaneously near to us and far from us (cf. Simmel, 1950) and we, in our relationship with another, may be both 'stranger' and 'friend' (Powdermaker, 1967). We may, as Greene (1973) indicates when speaking of the teacher as stranger, experience not just discomfort but a crisis. Greene refers to this as a crisis of confidence, but it can be much more than that; we can experience a 'dark night of the soul', where everything appears to break down, where some of our most cherished assumptions about ourselves and the world are torn apart. From such harrowing experiences there can, nonetheless, be a kind of educative healing – a sense, in time, of renewal. We may go on from a crisis that seems to cut to the heart of our existence to accomplish tasks that hitherto seemed impossible. The stranger who plays a part in creating a sense of despair for us can also provide the basis for a robust, realistic sense of hope that will serve us well in future endeavours.

The stranger presents to us as someone who invites us to think again about who we are and why we are here. But, as already noted, the invitation will not always be gentle, and it will seldom be extended at our convenience. It may be offered when we least expect it, heightening the sense of strangeness in the moment of the first encounter and demanding more of us subsequently. A stranger can prompt us to engage in a period of deep reflection, with no ready, quick-fix answers in sight. Making ourselves the subjects who are taught in such encounters will often involve a radical reconfiguration of traditional pedagogical relationships. The young can teach the old; the unqualified can offer something to those who are regarded as experts in their fields. We need not self-consciously adopt the posture of the student in order to be taught. Sometimes we will be 'taught a lesson' by a stranger whether we want this or not. There are good educational and ethical grounds, however, for opening ourselves up to the possibility of learning from strangers when they do appear. For such encounters may be precisely what is needed if we are to gain insights that would otherwise be obscured – by prejudice, habit or ignorance. An educative stance welcoming of the stranger is thus one that is not only characterised by openness but also humility. Recognising that there is much that we do not know, including not just content knowledge but also other ways of knowing and being, is essential if we are to be open to what strangers might have to offer.

One of the most firmly established commitments we often have in educational institutions – particularly at the tertiary level – is our faith in the value and power of reason. Those of us who teach in universities typically place a premium on the importance of rational argument and debate. We seek to develop our ideas in a logical manner, and we encourage the students with whom we work to do likewise. We strive for coherence, cohesiveness and rigour. We want to not merely give opinions or express our feelings on the political problems of the day; we must explain, elaborate and justify our views. Reason is the bedrock on which all serious scholarship is supposed to exist. An encounter with those who appear lacking in their rational capacities, or unwilling to develop or demonstrate them, can be disruptive and unsettling. It may at times be somewhat irritating, particularly where earnest attempts are being made to advance understanding in addressing a complex social issue. This sense of frustration, perhaps even dismay, can be heightened in the so-called 'post-truth' world we now inhabit, where 'fake news' can be peddled, and lies readily accepted, via social media and other online avenues (see Ozolins, 2022). But there are also situations where disruptions to our usual expectations of reason can have educative value, enabling us to see ourselves, others and the world in a fresh light.[4] An encounter with a stranger who appears to be 'mad' – to have lost all sense of reason – can be deeply disturbing but also educative.[5] This is especially evident in the pedagogical opportunities that are opened up to us by perhaps the most famous of all 'mad' characters in fiction: Cervantes' Don Quixote. It is to this archetypal figure we now turn, with the aid of Miguel de Unamuno, Franz Kafka and a contemporary chronicler of the pessimistic spirit, Joshua Dienstag.

Reason, Madness and Education: Reading *Don Quixote* as a Pedagogical Text

The broad outline of *Don Quixote* (Cervantes, 2005), first published in Spanish in the early seventeenth century and with numerous translations into other languages subsequently, is well known. This is a story about a man who, after immersing himself in fictional tales of chivalry, decides to take on the role of

---

4   On education, art and the limits of reason, see Baldacchino (2012); Roberts and Freeman-Moir (2013) and Roberts and Saeverot (2018).
5   Conceptions of madness (and responses to it) have, of course, changed over the centuries. In the contemporary world, the term is sometimes avoided altogether. It is certainly the case that the range of recognised psychiatric conditions has expanded dramatically since Cervantes' time. For one well-known historical and philosophical account of madness, see Foucault (2001). On madness in literature, see Shuger (2012).

knight errant for himself. With a family name that may have been Quixada, Quexada or Quexana (the narrator leaves this uncertain), he christens himself *Don Quixote of La Mancha* and enlists a poor local farmer, Sancho Panza, as his squire. Together the two men wander the Spanish countryside, administering their services to the many varied characters they encounter along the way. As the action in the novel unfolds, it becomes clear that Don Quixote has lost his mind. He tilts at windmills as if they are assailants; in an inn, he sees a castle. He is propelled by a romantic vision (inspired by his 'lady' Dulcinea) that seems to have little connection with reality, and he sees a logic behind his actions that is obvious to him alone. He delivers flowery, moralistic speeches that could have been lifted from the works of fiction he has ingested and is often unaware of what others around him are saying or doing. At times he loses his temper with Sancho, and he demands much of his overworked horse, Rocinante. He has little regard for his own safety. There are violent exchanges with other groups and individuals. His attempts to look the part in dressing and equipping himself as a knight errant are comical. Don Quixote is mocked and manipulated by others, but he retains his own sense of purpose and direction throughout. He eventually returns to his home in La Mancha, weakens and dies, recovering his reason in his final days.[6]

Don Quixote is a multi-layered work that lends itself well, despite (or perhaps because of) its considerable length, to repeated readings. The book we now know as *Don Quixote* was composed in two parts. Cervantes published the second part a decade after the first, as a response to the release of a false *Quixote* by a literary imposter.[7] Across the two parts, there are stories within stories. Cervantes appears to have grown with his two key characters, who both change, in their own distinctive ways, as the narrative progresses. The book is episodic in its approach to charting the adventures of Don Quixote and Sancho Panza, with a number of digressions and distractions but an abiding concern with the fate of the knight and his squire. It is a work filled with humour and sadness.[8] There is despair in its pages but also hope. Its influence has been immense. Among thinkers in the Continental tradition, it has left

---

6   On the historical and contemporary significance of *Don Quixote*, see Bandera (2006) and Bayliss (2006). In considering how the novel might be taught, adapted and applied in different settings, see Boyle and Hall (2016); Lathey (2012) and Miñana (2011).

7   This had a direct bearing on the fate of Don Quixote. According to Lathrop (2010, p. 18), 'Cervantes realized that he had to have his hero die at the end of the book so that no one else could try to continue his own hero's adventures'.

8   For an analysis of the humour in the work, see Hart (2009).

a particularly strong impression. Kierkegaard, in *Fear and Trembling* (Kierkegaard, 2005), reflects on the path taken by the 'knight of faith'. In a later book, *Concluding Unscientific Postscript* (Kierkegaard, 2009), he refers directly to Don Quixote when discussing subjective and objective approaches to truth. *Don Quixote* appears more than once in Schopenhauer's magnum opus, *The World as Will and Representation* (Schopenhauer, 1966). The spell cast by Cervantes is also evident in the work of Nietzsche, particularly in *The Gay Science* (Nietzsche, 1974). Dostoevsky likewise had a profound respect for Cervantes' achievement. 'Holy fools' feature regularly in the novels of his maturity, and there is throughout his work a sharp awareness of the limits of reason (Roberts & Saeverot, 2018). Don Quixote finds Russian literary cousins in the Underground Man (Dostoevsky, 2004), Prince Myshkin (Dostoevsky, 2001) and the Ridiculous Man (Dostoevsky, 1997). Sartre, Beauvoir and Camus were all familiar with Cervantes' literary creation. Perhaps the greatest admirer of all, however, was Cervantes' countryman, Miguel de Unamuno.[9]

Unamuno had a deep love for the figure of Don Quixote. The influence of the knight errant is evident in both his fiction (Unamuno, 1996, 2000) and his non-fiction (Unamuno, 1972). Unamuno felt that in Don Quixote, there was all of Spain, all of that which makes us distinctively human. For Unamuno, Don Quixote lived beyond even his own creator, beyond the world as we know it. From Don Quixote we have, eternally, Quixotism, and in Quixotism, Unamuno argues, we find 'a whole method, a whole epistemology, a whole aesthetic, a whole logic, a whole ethic, above all, a whole religion, that is to say, a total economy of the eternal and the divine, a total hope in the rationally absurd' (Unamuno, 1972, pp. 252–253). At first glance, this assessment may seem completely 'over the top', granting to a work of fiction far more philosophical and spiritual substance than is there. But Unamuno did not make such claims lightly. His thoughts are offered in the final chapter of his principal philosophical work, *The Tragic Sense of Life in Men and Nations*, and this is no accident. For Unamuno, Don Quixote allows us to go to the heart of the tragic nature of our existence. In Don Quixote, we can see that the tension between our desire for immortality and our capacity for critical reason will never be resolved. For Unamuno, consciousness is a 'disease', but as human beings we must learn to live with this. Attempts to prove the existence of God or the

---

9 For a helpful discussion of connections between Kierkegaard, Unamuno and the Knight of Faith, see Evans (2006). Unamuno's debt to Don Quixote is also evident in Yorba-Gray (2005).

reality of life beyond death through rational means are, in Unamuno's view, futile. Faith and reason are fundamentally opposed to each other. We must accept that we will continue to want to live on while recognising that from a rational point of view, this is an absurdity. Hope for us, as tragic souls tortured by the very qualities that make us distinctively human, lies in the uncertainty that remains about that which can never be fully known. We can, Unamuno reminds us, live with commitment and integrity, as if we will go on for ever, even if we are not certain that this is the case.

The Don Quixote of the novel recovers his reason in order to die, but there is, Unamuno suggests, a 'real' Don Quixote who lives on beyond this, among us all. It is not the return of Don Quixote's reason or his death that makes him immortal; it is his madness. This is what separates him most from us, but it is also what draws us closer to him. Don Quixote 'made himself ridiculous' (p. 350) but his ridiculousness is our own.[10] He sacrificed himself, it might be said, in order that we might better understand ourselves. He knows who he is and remains committed to his ideals, fighting desperately against the conflicting tendencies within himself. It is possible to see his immortality as merely the exchange of one form of madness for another: in closing the door on his escapades, and in regaining his reason at the last, Don Quixote goes off on another adventure, into the madness of the unknown that is death.[11] The Don Quixote that is with us to this day may have emerged from the comic figure of Cervantes' novel, but his real battle is with the despair we all must face. Don Quixote demonstrates, for all who pay close attention to him, the tragic nature of human existence. The tension between faith, feeling and wanting on the one hand and reason, intellect and questioning on the other is always there, even if in the figure of Don Quixote the balance seems, for much of Cervantes' novel, to tip heavily in one direction. Don Quixote's existence may be tragic, but it is not without hope; far from it. Despair is often conceived as the absence of hope, but Unamuno knows otherwise: 'it is despair and despair alone which engenders heroic hope, absurd hope, mad hope' (p. 352). Don Quixote stands opposed to 'modern, scientific, inquisitorial orthodoxy'; his quest is to rebuild a 'new and impossible Middle Ages, dualistic, contradictory, impassioned' (p. 354). His mission, Unamuno proclaims, is to 'cry aloud', to struggle and search in the wilderness, finding few listeners among men and women but a

---

10 As Cummings (2017, p. 141) points out, 'Unamuno is a philosopher who appears to accept the fact-value dichotomy, while insisting on the ultimate meaningfulness of human values, even when in direct conflict with the facts'.
11 Further reflections on death in *Don Quixote* can be found in Triplette (2019).

welcoming home in the forest, with a voice that falls to the ground like a seed that will one day grow into a giant cedar, singing 'an eternal hosanna to the Master of life and of death' (pp. 357–358).

Joshua Dienstag, in his study of pessimistic thought (Dienstag, 2006), views the novel through an educational lens. Dienstag argues that Don Quixote exemplifies the quest for the 'fearful and questionable' advocated by Nietzsche. Quixote transforms himself and, having done so, embarks on a journey that will allow those he encounters along the way to transform themselves. Against conventional standards, Dienstag concedes, his quest might be deemed a failure. Yet when his effect on others is examined, he is, in his own limited way, successful. Quixote's madness may be readily apparent to all who meet him, but there are, as Dienstag points out, numerous cases of characters in the novel who either end up adopting his view of the world or come to see the value of not disabusing him of his ideas. 'Even when they do not adopt his goals', Dienstag observes, 'they come to admire his example, as does the reader'. Quixote's presence has 'a liberating effect on those with whom he comes into contact, even if after being liberated they do not follow him' (p. 203). Cervantes' vision is, Dienstag contends, a pessimistic one, but his posture is not one of resignation: 'he has no particular hope of reforming the dismal and corrupt world into which he was born; he seeks only to resist and survive it, and to do so with a modicum of dignity and self-respect' (p. 205). Don Quixote's quest may seem futile, but it provides a means for coping with a world that is chaotic and unpredictable. As a knight errant, Quixote's hopes of building a better world are eventually dashed. This does not mean his quest has no educative value: '[I]f the narratives of chivalry that Cervantes mocks have been a dubious education for Quixote, *that is not at all the case for Quixote's own narrative of chivalry*, which is an education for Sancho Panza and, through him, for the rest of us' (p. 205).

Don Quixote raises questions about books and their potential influence on us as readers. Cervantes regarded the books of chivalry that had become popular in Spain during his lifetime as 'detestable' and felt their effects on the public would be highly undesirable (Dienstag, 2006, p. 206). It was, Cervantes makes clear, Don Quixote's voracious reading of these chivalrous tales that led to his madness. And yet, 'miraculously, by the end of the book, Don Quixote, for all his craziness, has come to seem one of the saner people in the jaded, unsentimental, early modern Spain that the novel depicts' (p. 206). If this is the case, it can be argued that Cervantes has a pedagogical purpose: he means, 'through the figure of Don Quixote, to educate us' (p. 206). Don Quixote is arguably transformed, but in what ways? It is not a straightforward situation of Don Quixote becoming a 'better person' – that is, more virtuous – for we are informed at the start of the novel that he was already known as 'Alonso the Good' (p. 212). Rather, his transformation is 'from a man who sat quietly at home and read books to one who felt it necessary to travel the world, seeking out injustice and correcting it' (p. 212). From his immersion in stories of chivalry, Don Quixote learns '*not* what to believe, but how to act and, more importantly, *that* he must act' (pp. 212–213). Thus, as Dienstag sees it, Don Quixote's educational significance lies in how he 'lives out' the narratives he encounters in books of chivalry; he becomes 'the author of his own actions' (p. 213). Cervantes shows that we can teach others, or provide something that is helpful for them to learn, even if our actions may at first seem baffling, or deserving of ridicule, to others. As is most evident in Sancho's development, 'Quixote does not persuade anyone of the validity of his ideas, but rather inspires their imitation of his example' (p. 214). Both of Cervantes' central characters come to know who they are, and both undergo a process of education (pp. 214–215).

Franz Kafka, himself the creator of one of the most memorable stories of strangeness in *The Metamorphosis* (Kafka, 1996), provides a distinctive perspective on *Don Quixote*, radically altering our view of the two key characters in the novel: 'Sancho Panza – who, by the way, has never boasted of it – by providing a great quantity of chivalrous romances by evening and by night, managed so successfully in the course of the years to get his devil, whom he later named Don Quixote, off his back, that the latter, all stability lost, went and performed the craziest deeds' (Kafka, 2012, p. 185). Don Quixote's strange behaviour, Kafka reassures us, was not directed at anything in particular and proved itself to be harmless. Sancho was a 'free man' who 'followed Don Quixote with equanimity and perhaps from a certain sense of responsibility on all his campaigns, deriving from them great and profitable entertainment from them till his end' (p. 185). Kafka's interpretation casts Sancho in a fresh light, moving him from the role of faithful squire to centre stage as the conductor of his own literary symphony.[12]

Sancho undergoes a process of educational – and *educative* – transformation, but this is no quick affair; rather, it takes place over many years. Sancho begins, if we are to believe the narrator, as 'a good man … but without much in the way of brains' (Cervantes, 2005, p. 55). In accepting the role of squire

---

12 Sancho Panza's manipulation of Don Quixote is also apparent in the novel. See Williamson (2015).

to Don Quixote, he is lured by the promise of becoming governor of an *ínsula* (island). After many adventures together, and against all expectations, he is granted his wish and governs with surprising subtlety, moderation and insight. He makes sensible decisions and takes appropriate action in negotiating the challenges of political life. Sancho gives up his governorship, but his development continues until his death. If Kafka's interpretation is followed, it is clear that Sancho wields the power he has over his creation – Don Quixote – with the same sense of care and fair-mindedness he exhibited in governing. He gains pleasure from his creative endeavours, but not, it might be said, at the expense of the dignity of Don Quixote. We do not have to go as far as Kafka has here to appreciate the pedagogical importance of Sancho Panza in Cervantes' novel. Sancho's education is also, as Dienstag (2006) notes, *our* education, and we learn with him and from him as he accompanies Don Quixote on his adventures, regardless of whether those escapades were his own creation or the product of Cervantes' literary imagination.

So, what kind of stranger is Don Quixote, and how might an encounter with him be educative for us as contemporary readers on Cervantes' novel? Don Quixote seems, at first glance, to be utterly separate from us, in another world as we might say. Apart from his brief return to sanity just before his death, he appears to dwell in a realm that is unreachable and unfathomable for any 'reasonable' or 'educated' person. There is, as the narrator in Lima Barreto's (2011) *The Sad End of Policarpo Quaresma* points out, something deeply saddening in such situations. An encounter with someone in a state of madness leaves us feeling disturbed, without knowing quite why this is the case. Madness seems to come from 'something that is stronger than we are' (p. 173). '[W]hen we hear a madman raving', *The Sad End of Policarpo Quaresma* continues, 'we are overcome by a sensation that he is not the one who is speaking – It is someone else, seeing for him, interpreting for him, someone who is there behind him, invisible!' (p. 173). It is the severing of the possibility of communication that constitutes the ultimate sadness in an encounter with madness, and this has important educational implications.[13] The ideal of educative dialogue, for example, typically presupposes the existence of two or more rational agents, with the capacity to engage in shared, meaningful conversation. Madness of the kind exhibited by Don Quixote creates a seemingly insurmountable barrier to the thoughtful exchange of views we seek to establish in pedagogical contexts. It is true that Sancho's banter with Don Quixote is one of the

---

13 This idea is developed at greater length in Roberts (2022a).

highlights of Cervantes' novel, but there is always something missing in the knight errant's role as a participant in these conversations. Sancho may be portrayed as a simple man, but it is he who must indulge Don Quixote's fantasies, allowing the latter to sustain a narrative that might otherwise be shattered by the many trials and tribulations they face in their adventures together. Sancho is *with* Don Quixote, but he cannot *be* Don Quixote; he can never fully grasp what goes on inside the knight errant's mind. If this is the case for Sancho, Don Quixote's closest, most loyal companion, what hope is there for us? Don Quixote will be forever 'off limits' to us – forever a stranger.

Unamuno's reference to despair in describing Don Quixote is, for us as readers, also *our* despair. This is Unamuno's great insight: we are, as beings compelled to live with the tragic tension between our vital and our rational tendencies, *all* fellow human sufferers, even though we may respond to this underlying sense of despair in different ways (Roberts, 2016). But in other ways too, it becomes apparent, on closer examination, that Don Quixote is not as far removed from us as we might think. There may be limits to the forms of dialogical communication we might enact, or contribute to, with someone like Don Quixote but that does not mean there cannot be a sense of connection. We might, indeed, conceive of this as a form of solidarity. Don Quixote presents himself to us as a stranger, distant in place and time, fictional rather than real and with a construction of reality that bears little resemblance to our own. But this does not mean we cannot relate to *some* of his thoughts and feelings and actions, some of his hopes and dreams, some of his weaknesses and vulnerabilities.[14] Don Quixote may remain unknowable to us, but that is arguably the case for all others we encounter in pedagogical situations – indeed, in life more generally. It is just that in Don Quixote's case, his 'unknowability' is of an extreme kind. This need not hinder the possibility of feeling a sense of solidarity with him. To the contrary, by depicting Don Quixote as apparently so 'far gone' in his command over his rational faculties, Cervantes prompts reflection on the part of the reader, encouraging us to make comparisons that unveil more than we initially expect. This can be an uncomfortable process, but, as has been argued elsewhere in this book, discomfort is sometimes necessary if educational progress is to be made.

---

14 If we are to make such connections when encountering the strange in works of art, we arguably need to attain a certain kind of distance from our own everyday concerns. This is consistent with Greene's approach to aesthetic education (see Pinar, 2011, pp. 101–102).

If we keep Unamuno in mind, what is significant is Don Quixote's declaration that *he* knows who he is.[15] *He* has a sense of his own identity and purpose. He exists not just for others but in the service of something higher – something noble and enduring and worthwhile. Don Quixote pursues his ideals with a passion – a distorted, misguided passion perhaps, but one that is no less important for that. Don Quixote lives, as Kierkegaard's (2009) Climacus would say, *his* truth, a truth that matters to him, with integrity and commitment.[16] His truth may be out of kilter with 'objective' reality, but in committing himself to his ideals, he is true to himself. The sense of connection we can build with Don Quixote does not consist in trying to uncover all his layers, with a view to revealing the 'real' Alonso the Good behind the fantasy that is the adventurous knight errant. Cervantes ensures that this will remain a mystery for us. What we can 'know' is that if Don Quixote wandered into a school or university classroom today, we would instantly recognise him as a fellow human being. He would suffer, as we all do, from the tragic tension Unamuno identifies. He has thoughts, wants and feelings. He is shaped by his relationships with others. He attempts to make sense of the world, even if he does so very much in his own idiosyncratic manner. He may be defined forever, as a literary creation, by his madness – his perplexing strangeness – but it is still very much a *human* madness. If he stood before us, our first obligation would be to acknowledge him – to pay attention to him, not as an abstraction but as a distinctive individual. He would be worthy of our attention simply because he exists, and from this starting point the possibilities for an educative encounter with this stranger begin to take shape and expand.[17]

Implications for the Classroom

We seldom stop to think about how important the figure of the stranger is in the contemporary world. We are surrounded by strangers. Of the billions of people on planet Earth, the vast majority will be strangers for us. Some of us know more people than others, but in most cases our relationships with others – through family, social or professional connections – will not extend beyond a few dozen, perhaps a few hundred, people. It is true that in the age

---

15 See further, Martinez (2016).
16 Cf. Ziolkowski (1992); see further, Roberts (2023).
17 The notion of attention, as employed here, can be traced back to the work of Simone Weil (1997, 2001, 2002) and Iris Murdoch (2001).

of social media, some public figures may have thousands, possibly millions, of Internet 'friends'. But a click on a keyboard does not constitute a relationship, and the connections between 'stars' and 'fans' are for the most part relatively tenuous; the millions of followers amount to millions of strangers. In the physical world, we encounter strangers all the time, sometimes exchanging a few words, sometimes merely nodding our heads, often making no gestures at all. Strangers are everywhere in education as well. Most who are involved in teaching, in early childhood centres, schools, universities or other institutions, greet a new group of strangers each year or every semester. The task of engaging with the stranger, as a professional responsibility, is thus a perpetually renewed challenge. For many students, the teacher will also be a stranger to them. What is demanded of us, then, as teachers and learners, in facing the other who is – and who may or may not remain – a stranger? There is, of course, no one best way to answer this question, but some possibilities are prefigured in the comments on Greene's work earlier in this chapter and in the analysis of Don Quixote above.

In developing her notion of the teacher as stranger, Greene employs the helpful analogy of a person returning home after a period away and having to readjust to what in the past would have felt familiar. We can also consider our pedagogical obligations by contemplating a similar scenario, but from a different standpoint. These days, the figure of the stranger is often portrayed in a negative light. Children are taught to develop an awareness of 'stranger danger', and in the murky world of the Internet it is possible for strangers to hide behind a veil of anonymity in making vitriolic comments about others. Online exchanges can be filled with hatred, fuelled by ignorance and prejudice, with those subject to attacks by Internet 'trolls' never being able to identify their abusers. Strangers are not infrequently regarded as a risk to our safety, security or well-being. Those from foreign lands may be positioned as a threat, even if the real dangers often exist much closer to home. To be a stranger, then, is, in many circumstances, to immediately be positioned as not only 'other' but as a potentially hostile, dangerous, repellent other. And yet, there is, for all of this, another way we can approach the stranger, in a manner connected with the 'homecoming' example provided by Greene. We can imagine someone who is not known to us as an individual, but about whom we may know something, turning up – though not unannounced – at our home. How might such a situation unfold?

Our obligation might first be to provide a welcoming presence for the other – the distinctive individual human being – we face at the door. We might greet our visitor with a smile and usher him or her into the dwelling. A handshake or some other form of culturally appropriate greeting might be offered. We may ask about the journey getting here, or comment on the weather, or make some other light conversation. The new acquaintance might be invited to sit down, and refreshments could be made available. This initial easing into the process of getting to know the stranger might lead into more substantial and detailed conversation, perhaps over a shared meal. The awkwardness or nervousness that may be evident early on in the encounter could give way to a more relaxed, free-flowing, engaging exchange of ideas as the conversation progresses. At the end of the visit, the stranger is, in some senses at least, a stranger no more. If the interactions between those involved go well, both the visitor and the visited will have gained something worthwhile from the gathering – perhaps some new insight about a form of experience the other may have had, or a better understanding of an occupation or interest or area of study, or a fresh perspective on a social or political issue. From a meeting of this kind there may emerge a better appreciation, however small, for another way of being in the world.

This is not too dissimilar to what might reasonably be expected in a classroom situation. Students taking a course at university or a subject at school may have gained indirect knowledge of their teacher via reports from others, or in reading his or her work, or through listening to what he or she has had to say in other contexts. The teacher will thus often not be a complete stranger, but there will still be much to learn in appreciating what he or she can offer to them. For a teacher, it is possible that some of the students will be known from previous classes, but many will not. A 'class' of students is, however, not merely an amorphous mass of bodies to whom content must be imparted; each student will, as an individual, have his or her own unique background, personality traits, forms of previous experience, interests and inclinations. Those students who are not known to the teacher through previous classroom encounters are strangers who must, with others, be welcomed into the educational environment. There is in such situations considerable uncertainty about what the 'welcoming' process may involve, regardless of any institutional protocols that must be applied. Teachers can never know quite what will happen as they begin to share their knowledge, begin to interact with students, enter and re-enter the classroom each day. It is in this very unpredictability, this uncertainty, opened up by an encounter with strangers, that the space for education resides.

Approaching students as strangers, with the openness this requires, can, in a counter-intuitive way, diminish rather than exacerbate the distance between participants in an educational conversation. If a teacher brings the humility necessary to say, in effect, 'I do not know you; let me learn something from you', she or he is tacitly acknowledging that students, as strangers, can also be teachers. It is not that teachers and students become identical with each other; both retain their own distinctive responsibilities and are answerable to others in different ways. But there is in such an approach a recognition that strangeness can be educative. Strangeness, as experienced through our encounter with another human being or in other ways, can teach and can bring more to pedagogical situations than would otherwise be there. A sense of strangeness can be created via direct instruction, but it can also emerge via indirect pedagogies (Saeverot, 2013, 2022). Just as 'the stranger' must be distinguished from 'the other', so too must 'strangeness' be contrasted with 'difference'. The stranger may be an 'other' to us, but if so, this will be otherness of a quite specific kind. We may, moreover, encounter a stranger who is *not* 'other' to us, as in the experience (mentioned earlier) of living with 'the stranger within'. 'Difference' is typically applied as a category pertaining to human subjects; a sense of 'strangeness', by contrast, can be created in myriad ways, through encounters with other living beings but also through our reading of fiction, our watching of a film or our contemplation of a painting. An experience of the phenomenon of strangeness can occur in our physical activities, in our encounters with nature, in meditation or in sleep. We can set out to deliberately cultivate such experiences, but they can also occur in unexpected ways, at any time.

How does the stranger teach? It is not enough to say, by offering something 'different', for this simply invites further questions: Different from what or from whom? In what ways? The stranger teaches by allowing an other, or others, to experience a sense of strangeness. This experience need not be dramatic or shocking; it can be subtle, perhaps even barely detectable, but there nonetheless. We may only be able to comprehend the effects of an encounter with strangeness after the event has occurred, sensing at the time that something was 'not quite right' but only grasping why and how this was so later, on reflection and analysis. Perceptions of strangeness vary from person to person; the same stranger may teach different people in different ways. This is how we can view Don Quixote. He may know who he is, or claim to do so, but he remains a mystery to us – and to each of us in our own unique ways. The student as stranger teaches not necessarily by bringing content knowledge to the teacher or to his or her fellow students, or by setting out to disrupt expectations, or by drawing on life experiences he or she may have had that differ from those of others present in the classroom. Depending on what others bring to their encounter with the student, the student as stranger may teach by simply being there. This is not meant to suggest that the stranger, understood in these terms, becomes an object – something 'of use' to others. 'Being there' means being oneself, playing a part in creating the distinctive learning environment that is this classroom, with this group of people, at this time, in this place. This is not a denial of the subjectivity of the student but rather a recognition of what is required of the teacher if he or she is to also be taught. It is a way of acknowledging that what we bring to others allows them to teach us.

Conclusion

Reading *Don Quixote* and encountering a fictional character who appears to have lost all reason may seem a world away from a situation where a teacher is facing a group of students in a school classroom on a Monday morning. But in both cases, the pedagogical significance of strangeness can reveal itself to us, if we are sufficiently open, humble, curious and attentive in our stance toward others. The welcoming posture advocated here must, of course, be applied selectively and with appropriate care. Warnings about the potential dangers posed by strangers, in some contexts, are well placed and must be heeded. Each situation must be taken on its own merits, and those in positions of responsibility – including teachers – must exercise appropriate caution in the advice they give to others. Behaviours in the classroom will be subject to professional codes of conduct, but beyond those formal requirements there are also ethical standards that all thoughtful, committed teachers will want to apply for themselves. These caveats are important, but they need not deter us from taking the role of the stranger, and the experience of strangeness, more seriously in our educational endeavours. In an age obsessed with measuring and managing everything, experiences that disrupt the order we seek can be liberating; they can wake us up from the sleep that can be induced when we are hypnotised by numbers, by data, by rankings and ratings.[18] Numbers bring a false sense of security, masking the subtleties, the deviations, the complexities that give pedagogical situations their true value. Teachers who make themselves students of strangeness relinquish some control over the teaching process but can become better teachers for that – more sensitive, more creative, more adaptable to changing circumstances and situations.

---

18 See further, Roberts (2022b).

Meeting a stranger takes courage, not just in dealing with the nervousness that often characterises initial encounters, but in being prepared for the unexpected in what follows. Calmness and patience are needed if we are to allow the stranger to speak to us, not just with words but through his or her actions, gestures and silences. As Unamuno observed, it is Don Quixote's 'madness' that remains with us long after we have finished reading Cervantes' novel. We continue to think about Don Quixote – his strange way of seeing the world, his interactions with Sancho Panza, his bizarre actions and pronouncements, his unswerving commitment to his truth and his ideals – at moments and in places and situations far removed from the world he occupies. Don Quixote unsettles and disturbs his readers. And yet, it is in his very ridiculousness, his unknowability, that his role as a teacher emerges. We sense there is something more to be known and thus reach out to this fictional stranger; Don Quixote sets a task for us as learners. His strangeness invites us to peer more closely, not just at him, but at ourselves. Don Quixote, precisely by being so ridiculous, prompts us to think again about what we regard as rational, about how we make the different parts of our world sensible and coherent and bearable. Don Quixote does not need to be 'explained' or 'justified'; he offers himself to us, as readers through the generations, as a gift – as a stranger who teaches, without expecting anything in return. Teachers and students in the classrooms of today can continue to learn from his example, without in any way seeking to emulate his deeds or inhabit his perplexing inner world. They can be strangers for each other, always 'coming home', as Maxine Greene might have put it, to embrace the unexpected, disorderly, infinitely rewarding possibilities for educative experience.

References

Baldacchino, J. (2012). *Art's way out: Exit pedagogy and the cultural condition*. Sense.

Baldacchino, J. (2017). Freedom, aesthetics, and the agôn of living in Maxine Greene's philosophy. *Review of Education, Pedagogy, and Cultural Studies*, 39(1), 18–38.

Bandera, C. (2006). *The humble story of Don Quixote: Reflections on the birth of the modern novel*. Catholic University of America Press.

Barreto, L. (2011). *Triste fim de Policarpo Quaresma / The sad end of Policarpo Quaresma* (M. Carlyon, Trans.). Instituto Cultural Cidade Viva.

Bayliss, R. (2006). What *Don Quixote* means (today). *Comparative Literature Studies*, 43(4), 382–397.

Beauvoir, S. de (1992). *All men are mortal* (L. M. Friedman, Trans.). W. W. Norton.

Boyle, M. & Hall, C. (2016). Teaching *Don Quixote* in the digital age: Page and screen, visual and tactile. *Hispania*, 99(4), 600–614.
Camus, A. (1989). *The stranger* (M. Ward, Trans.). Vintage.
Cervantes, M. de (2005). *Don Quixote* (E. Grossman, Trans.). Vintage.
Cummings, A. (2017). Don Quixote meets Mr Gradgrind: A neglected proof for immortality. *Logos: A Journal of Catholic Thought and Culture*, 20(1), 135–156.
Dienstag, J. F. (2006). *Pessimism: Philosophy, ethic, spirit*. Princeton University Press.
Dostoevsky, F. (1997). The dream of a ridiculous man. In F. Dostoevsky, *The eternal husband and other stories* (R. Pevear & L. Volokhonsky, Trans.) pp. 296–319. Bantam Books.
Dostoevsky, F. (2001). *The idiot* (R. Pevear & L. Volokhonsky, Trans.). Granta.
Dostoevsky, F. (2004). *Notes from underground* (R. Pevear & L. Volokhonsky, Trans.). Everyman's Library.
Evans, J. E. (2006). Kierkegaard, Unamuno, and Don Quijote as the Knight of Faith. *Symposium*, 60(1), 3–16.
Foucault, M. (2001). *Madness and civilization*. Routledge.
Greene, M. (1973). *Teacher as stranger*. Wadsworth.
Greene, M. (1995). *Releasing the imagination: Essays on education, the arts, and social change*. Jossey-Bass.
Greene, M. (2018). *Landscapes of learning*. Teachers College Press.
Hart, T. R. (2009). What's funny about *Don Quixote*? *Hispanic Research Journal*, 10(3), 227–232.
Kafka, F. (1996). *The metamorphosis* (S. Corngold, Trans.). W. W. Norton.
Kafka, F. (2012). *A hunger artist and other stories* (J. Crick, Trans.). Oxford University Press.
Kierkegaard, S. (2005). *Fear and trembling* (A. Hannay, Trans.). Penguin.
Kierkegaard, S. (2009). *Concluding unscientific postscript* (A. Hannay, Trans.). Cambridge University Press.
Lathey, G. (2012). "Places to which I have never been": *Don Quixote*, the childhood imagination, and English-language adaptations for young readers. *Hispanic Research Journal*, 13(3), 195–217.
Lathrop, T. (2010). *Don Quixote* and its errant author. *New England Review*, 31(4), 8–19.
Miñana, R. (2011). "The Don Quixote of the streets": Social justice theater in São Paulo, Brazil. *Cervantes*, 31(1), 159–170.
Martinez, F. (2016). "I know who I am": Don Quixote, self-fashioning, and the humanness of ordinary identity. *Philosophy and Literature*, 40(2), 511–525.
Murdoch, I. (2001). *The sovereignty of good*. Routledge.
Nietzsche, F. (1974). *The gay science* (W. Kaufmann, Trans.). Vintage Books.
Ozolins, J. (Ed.). (2022). *Education in an age of lies and fake news: Regaining a love of truth*. Routledge.
Pinar, W. F. (Ed.). (1998). *The passionate mind of Maxine Greene*. Routledge.
Pinar, W. F. (2011). *The character of curriculum studies: Bildung, currere, and the recurring question of the subject*. Palgrave Macmillan.
Powdermaker, H. (1967). *Stranger and friend*. W. W. Norton.
Roberts, P. (2013). The stranger within: Dostoevsky's underground. *Educational Philosophy and Theory*, 45(4), 396–408.

Roberts, P. (Ed.). (2015). *Shifting focus: Strangers and strangeness in literature and education*. Routledge.
Roberts, P. (2016). *Happiness, hope, and despair: Rethinking the role of education*. Peter Lang.
Roberts, P. (2022a). *Paulo Freire: Philosophy, pedagogy, and practice*. Peter Lang.
Roberts, P. (2022b). *Performativity, politics and education: From policy to philosophy*. Brill.
Roberts, P. (2023). Education, truth and subjectivity: Revisiting Kierkegaard. *Oxford Review of Education, 49*(3), 376–389.
Roberts, P. & Freeman-Moir, J. (2013). *Better worlds: Education, art, and utopia*. Lexington Books.
Roberts, P. & Saeverot, H. (2018). *Education and the limits of reason: Reading Dostoevsky, Tolstoy and Nabokov*. Routledge.
Saeverot, H. (2013). *Indirect pedagogy. Some lessons in existential education*. Sense Publishers.
Saeverot, H. (2022). *Indirect education: Exploring indirectness in teaching and research*. Routledge.
Schopenhauer, A. (1966). *The world as will and representation* (E. F. Payne, Trans.). Dover.
Shuger, D. (2012). *Don Quixote in the archives: Madness and literature in early modern Spain*. Edinburgh University Press.
Simmel, G. (1950) The stranger. In *The sociology of Georg Simmel* (K. Wolff, Trans.), pp. 402–408. The Free Press.
Triplette, S. (2019) Death and ritual in *Don Quixote*. *Cervantes, 39*(1), 201–217.
Unamuno, M. de (1972). *The tragic sense of life in men and nations* (A. Kerrigan, Trans.). Princeton University Press.
Unamuno, M. de (1996). *Abel Sanchez and other stories* (A. Kerrigan, Trans.). Regnery Publishing.
Unamuno, M. de (2000). *Mist: A tragicomic novel* (W. Fite, Trans.). University of Illinois Press.
Weil, S. (1997). *Gravity and grace* (A. Wills, Trans.). Bison Books.
Weil, S. (2001). *Waiting for God* (E. Craufurd, Trans.). Perennial Classics.
Weil, S. (2002). *The need for roots* (A. Wills, Trans.). Routledge Classics.
Williamson, E. (2015). The Devil in *Don Quixote*. *Bulletin of Spanish Studies, 92*(8–10), 147–166.
Yorba-Gray, G. B. (2005). Don Quixote till kingdom come: The (un)realized eschatology of Miguel de Unamuno. *Christianity and Literature, 54*(2), 165–182.
Ziolkowski, E. (1992). Don Quixote and Kierkegaard's understanding of the single individual in society. In G. B. Connell & C. S. Evans (Eds.), *Foundations of Kierkegaard's vision of community: Religion, ethics, and politics in Kierkegaard* (pp. 130–143). Humanities Press International.

· 5 ·

EDUCATION, DEATH AND IMMORTALITY: FROM UNAMUNO TO BEAUVOIR AND BEYOND

In the West, there is a long tradition of philosophical interest in the question of death. Our understanding of death, many have recognised, can have a significant bearing on how we see ourselves as human beings. It can shape our sense of who we are, why we are here and what we should do with our lives. Death is a complicated, multi-layered, 'charged' topic, and it must be approached with sensitivity and care. We often associate death and dying with sadness and grief, sometimes with great suffering and struggle. The death of a family member or close friend can be particularly harrowing, but we may also be profoundly disturbed by other losses (e.g. of human lives through famine or war, or of animal lives through environmental destruction). Talking about death – even thinking about it – is always a risky process. There is merit nonetheless in examining this most difficult of subjects a little more closely than is often the case, and precedents for doing so have been set for thousands of years.[1]

---

1 This chapter was first presented as a Keynote Address at the Philosophy of Education Society of Great Britain annual conference in Oxford, 22–24 March 2024. Thanks are due to the conference convenors for the invitation to speak at this event and to other delegates who asked helpful questions and offered thoughtful comments.

Socrates, with his argument for the immortality of the human soul (as captured in Plato's *Phaedo*), provides a common starting point for inquiries in this domain. His calm acceptance of his own death at the hands of the Athenian authorities in 399 B.C. was premised on the view that the body, with its impulses and desires, is an impediment to the development of reason; in death, Socrates wagered, the separation of the soul from these distracting influences finds its fulfilment. There is thus, from a Socratic point of view, nothing to fear in death (Plato, 2003). Similar reassurances were provided by other thinkers in antiquity but on different philosophical grounds. The Epicureans, for instance, adopted the position that death should be 'nothing' for us, arguing that just as our non-existence in the long period before we were born was of no concern to us, so too should our non-existence after death not bother us (Lucretius, 1999, p. 92). The Stoics acknowledged that human life is 'treacherous' and 'deceptive' but maintained that the prospect of our demise need not add to our troubles; cultivating a sense of readiness for death, by constantly having it in mind, diminishes its hold over us (Seneca, 2007, p. 78).[2]

In these ancient schools of thought, philosophy was, according to Pierre Hadot, not merely a theoretical exercise but a *way of life*. Death was a central theme in this world and there was, from the beginning, an educational dimension to the work undertaken. Philosophy was seen as a form of preparation for death. In committing ourselves to a philosophical mode of life, we are 'learning to die' (Hadot, 1995, p. 93). For educationists, this notion is rich with possibilities for theoretical investigation. We might ask: What are the ontological, epistemological and ethical assumptions underpinning this ideal? What does it mean to 'learn' and to 'die'? How, when, where and with whom does this learning occur? How can teachers assist learners in this task? How might learning of this kind be compromised or constrained? To date, these questions and others relating to death and dying have received only limited attention in the international philosophy of education community. Recognition of the need for further work in this area appears to be growing, but in many respects this is a conversation that is only just beginning to get underway.[3]

---

2   Epictetus puts it this way: 'Let death be before your eyes every day, and you will never have any abject thought nor excessive desire' (cited in Hadot, 1995, p. 131).
3   Compare Arcilla (1997); Bertoldo (2023); Blacker (1998); Dahlbeck (2015); Dhillon (1997); Neiman (1997); Peters (2021); Puolimatka and Solasaari (2006); Roberts (2012); Roberts et al. (2023); Schwieler (2022); Shim (2020); Smeyers et al. (2007, Chapter 6) and van Kessel and Burke (2018). There is a well-established body of scholarship on 'death education' (Herrán Gascón et al., 2023), with an emphasis on the development, provision and evaluation

It is not just the case, as the ancients counselled, that philosophy can prepare us for death. The reverse is also true: death can prepare us for philosophy, and this too is very much an educational process (Roberts et al., 2023). In observing, acknowledging and anticipating death, we may be prompted to ask questions that might otherwise not have occurred to us. As we begin to take death seriously, we can find ourselves thinking more deeply about the nature of reality, time, being and nothingness. We may feel a need to read more widely or to reread texts we thought we already knew. Our attitudes towards the spiritual beliefs and cultural practices of different groups, past and present, may change. In reflecting on who or what dies, where, when and how, we can face uncomfortable moral dilemmas. Death, we quickly discover, is not merely personal but also political. Our sense of how we are connected to other forms of life on the planet may start to shift. This is not to suggest there is anything inevitable or uniform in the way death, having become a matter of greater concern, works on us. Nor should we see the forms of reflection engendered by a willingness to attend to death as at once disciplined philosophical inquiry. But bringing death into sharper focus can be an important part of a longer, more expansive, philosophical and educational journey.

There are many possible paths in undertaking such a journey, one of which centres on the prospect of immortality. This has often been connected – in religion as well as in philosophy and literature – with the question of what happens to us after we die, but immortality can also be conceived in a variety of other ways. With new developments in computing, medicine and biotechnology, discussions of different forms of survival after or without death have taken on fresh significance. One writer who is helpful in addressing questions relating to death and immortality is Miguel de Unamuno (1864–1936). Unamuno's deep longing to live on, eternally, as the man he was, provided the driving force behind much of his work. The theme of death is especially prominent in his philosophical magnum opus, *The Tragic Sense of Life* (Unamuno, 1972), but it also hovers over his contributions as a novelist and short story writer. Death, as Unamuno sees it, haunts almost everything else we do. Death makes its presence felt in the priorities we set for ourselves, the relationships we build and the decisions we make. For all of us, Unamuno claims, there is a fundamental drive to continue in some

---

of programmes on death and dying, particularly in the health sector. Work on death is also available in periodicals devoted to other areas of educational study, including environmental education (Affifi & Christie, 2019), educational policy studies (Johansson, 2022) and digital/post-digital education (Savin-Baden, 2019).

form. Even if we do not expect to survive beyond the death of our physical bodies, a desire for immortality expresses itself in other ways in our activities and commitments as human beings.

This chapter explores some of the implications of these ideas for education. It argues that while a wish to live on is evident in teaching, learning and research, not all forms of immortality are desirable. In making this argument, reference is made to Simone de Beauvoir's (1992) novel, *All Men Are Mortal*, and to recent social and technological trends. The chapter acknowledges the value of Unamuno's work, while also pointing to some of its limits. Implicit throughout is the idea that whatever our views on immortality, the problems posed by death warrant continuing reflection and discussion in education.

A Longing to Live On: The Work of Miguel de Unamuno

Anyone familiar with Miguel de Unamuno's work will know that he was obsessed with the problem of death. His focus in *The Tragic Sense of Life* is not on what death means for 'humanity' – an abstract category – but rather on its significance for the existing 'flesh and blood' individual; someone who is 'born, suffers, and dies' (Unamuno, 1972, p. 3). As individual human beings, we engage in distinctive forms of conscious activity. We have the capacity to think, to reflect and to ask questions. We can place ourselves on a larger historical plane, looking back at the past and imagining what might happen in the future. These capabilities open up creative possibilities for us that are denied other living creatures, but they can also be a source of anguish and despair. Consciousness is a 'disease' – but one we must learn to accommodate (p. 22). At the heart of the human condition, Unamuno argues, lies a tragic tension between our wants and feelings on the one hand and our critical reasoning consciousnesses on the other. Our deepest desire is to live on beyond death, but reason tells us that this is an impossibility. Unamuno found the prospect of a death that would result in nothingness – in the complete obliteration of his consciousness – utterly horrific. He admitted, with Kierkegaard, that 'if the mortality of the soul is terrifying, its immortality is no less so' (p. 136).[4] Yet he desperately wanted to continue living, not in some transformed state but as the

---

4   This is because 'even if we overcome reason by a powerful effort of faith, even if we overcome that reasoning which tells us and shows us that the soul is only a function of the physical organism, we must still wonder what an immortal and eternal life of the soul may

unique individual he was, and everything in him rebelled against the idea of death. The 'problem' of death for Unamuno, then, was not merely an intellectual one; it was very much a lived experience – a titanic inner struggle, with no apparent reconciliation between the competing impulses he recognised within himself.

Unamuno's preoccupation with death played itself out in his own life and in the characters he fashioned through his fictional work. The priest in the story *San Manuel Bueno, Martyr* (Unamuno, 1996), for example, confesses that he does not believe in God, but strives to shield the villagers he serves from his terrible secret, aware of their need for the consolation faith provides. Unamuno sees philosophy and religion as fundamentally at odds with each other. They are contradictory in their aims, methods and conclusions, but they also depend on each other. 'There is no religion', Unamuno maintains, 'without some philosophic basis, nor is there any philosophy without religious roots: each lives off its opposite' (Unamuno, 1972, p. 126). Unamuno *wanted* to believe in God, but was unable to unreservedly do so.[5] He took the view, however, that wanting to believe is the first step in believing; faith is a matter of will, not of reason. Unamuno did not definitively reject the idea of God, but neither could he simply accept church doctrine. His exact religious position remained ambiguous, but he can perhaps best be seen as an agnostic, admitting to his doubts and indeed cherishing them as the basis for an ethic of hope. The doubt he held dear was not the methodological scepticism of Descartes but passionate doubt: 'the eternal conflict between reason and feeling, between science and life, between the logical and the biotic' (p. 120). Unamuno could not understand those who claimed not to care whether there was life after death, describing such apparent indifference as monstrous. Neither, it must be pointed out, could he fathom those who believed without ever hearing the voice of doubt. Unamuno wanted to keep the tension at the heart of the human condition alive within himself, noting that while our reasoning consciousnesses lead us to despair, in despair we seek something more.

The yearning to live on may be so strong that it rides 'roughshod' over reason, but reason, Unamuno cautions, 'will have its revenge' (p. 127). Reason fights constantly to establish order, to explain and to control; faith and feeling fight back, seeking to make reason conform to our deepest desires. The

---

be'. This wondering, Unamuno concedes, 'involves a series of contradictions and absurdities' (p. 136).
5 For a detailed account of Unamuno's struggle to believe, see Evans (2013).

complete victory of reason – pure thought – would be suicide.[6] But thought, Unamuno reminds us, relies on a thinker – on a complex individual, situated in a time and place, who must make decisions and act – and because of this, reason is placed at the service of life, whether the thinker acknowledges this or not. We seek through reason what the heart wants, even if only indirectly and in ways we cannot understand ourselves. We may attempt to 'live on' in other ways – through our children or our work, for example – without always being aware of how or why we are doing so. We strive to give our lives meaning and significance, terrified, deep down, by the idea that we do not matter at all – by the thought that, ultimately, *nothing* matters. We cannot overcome this terror by denying the tensions within us; instead, we must learn to live with the dynamic interplay between these inner forces. From the clash between reason and desire arises uncertainty: 'holy, sweet, saving uncertainty, our supreme consolation' (p. 131). If we retain some doubt, we can live; we can give our lives a sense of purpose, hope and anticipation. But this will never be an entirely comfortable process. Any peace we achieve will be only temporary, and we must come to accept a certain restlessness as a defining feature of our existence. In struggling and striving we suffer, but we also create ourselves as human beings.

Suffering is often portrayed in a negative light, but from Unamuno's perspective, we need not see it this way. It is only through suffering – the 'substance of life' – that we become who we are as unique individuals (p. 224). Unamuno observes that even in moments of happiness, we often feel a 'touch of anguish' (p. 224). Those who appear not to suffer, who luxuriate in their good fortune, professing to be happy, seem in Unamuno's eyes to lack substance. They are 'usually incapable of loving or of being loved, and they go through life without any inner meaning' (p. 225). Love allows us to think and act in ways that transcend vanity and self-interest. Love is a shared expression of the longing for something eternal. There is, however, nothing 'easy' about love. True love,

---

6 This point in Unamuno's argument is also drawn from Kierkegaard, who explains: 'The Greek philosopher was one who exists, and did not forget that fact. He therefore resorted to suicide, or to dying from the world in the Pythagorean sense, or to being dead in a Socratic sense to be able to think. He was conscious of being a thinking being, but he was also conscious that existence, as his medium, by putting him in the constant course of becoming, prevented him from thinking all the time. So, to be able truly to think, he took his own life. Modern philosophy smiles loftily at such childishness, as though every modern thinker did not know, as well as he knows that thought and being are one, that to be what he thinks is not worth the effort' (Kierkegaard, 2009, pp. 258–259).

Unamuno argues, cannot exist without suffering; love is 'resigned despair' (p. 225). We want love and happiness, but we cannot have both; we must choose one or the other. In the suffering that is love, there remains the possibility of an 'uncertain hope' (p. 225). Despair is often conceived as the loss of hope, but Unamuno does not see it this way. It is from despair – *through* despair – that hope gains its significance and meaning (pp. 351–352). Love keeps us awake, in a state of anguish. But those who take the path of happiness, who feel satisfied, 'fall asleep in habit, near neighbor to annihilation'; they 'begin to cease to be' (p. 225). Our capacity for suffering, for anguish, makes us all the more human. This is what Unamuno wanted in living his philosophy: not to be transformed into some other state or form, or even to become a perfected version of the man he was, but to remain *himself* for all time. His words have become immortalised in his books, but he would have given them all away to *be* immortal – to live on, today, tomorrow and forever.

Education and Immortality

We have seen that for Unamuno, the desire to live on exerts a powerful influence over our activities as human beings. Even if we reject any notion of personal survival after death, this drive will manifest itself in other ways. In education, the quest for immortality takes a number of different forms. One example can be found in the act of teaching, and in particular in the desire to live on through the students with whom we work.[7] Many who enter the teaching profession do so because they wish to make a worthwhile difference in other lives. In building pedagogical relationships with students and in passing on what we know to them, we hope our teaching will, at least in some small way, make the world a better place. We trust that our commitment to others in educational environments will, in turn, bear fruit in the years ahead, perhaps not just in the students themselves but also in the people with whom they interact. Such sentiments may be reinforced by those who are taught. As adults, we can reflect on teachers we have encountered in the past and feel a sense of gratitude for what they have given to us. We can appreciate the mark they have left on our lives. The teacher's immortality resides in what the student becomes, in what is carried forward to future generations. There is seldom a sense of instant gratification here. A teacher's influence will not

---

[7] This idea is discussed at length in Blacker (1998), Roberts (2012) and van Kessel and Burke (2018).

always be easy to detect and may not be recognised or appreciated until many years later in a student's life. But for many teachers, the rewards associated with the vocation do not have to be immediate or quantifiable; there can be a quiet sense of satisfaction in knowing that something of themselves remains – something *good* – long after they have gone. The desire to live on in this way, while admirable in many respects, is not without its dangers. The ego may intrude inappropriately, shifting the focus too much from 'what is best for the student' to 'what pleases the teacher'. Exerting an influence can, under some circumstances, undermine the capacity students have to form their own views. Teachers can sometimes have difficulty accepting the fact that their sense of what is important – what is worth preserving – will not always be shared by others. They may not be able to see, in a sufficiently nuanced way, how their values differ from those embraced and enacted by others. And in focusing heavily on their relationships with students, they may end up downplaying the significance of the subject matter being taught.

Another example of seeking to live on can be found in the written work we produce. This applies mainly, though not exclusively, to those employed in tertiary education institutions. Motivations for writing and publishing vary and will often be influenced by the cultures of performativity that have become so entrenched in universities over recent decades.[8] But for many researchers, there is a hope that something of themselves will endure in the books, articles and chapters they write.[9] Where the research undertaken is primarily theoretical, as is the case in philosophy of education, the ideas developed in undertaking scholarly work become particularly important. Having 'something to say', and allowing that to be left as a statement from us after we are gone, can be a quiet driver behind our writing activities. Of course, knowing quite what that is may not be immediately evident to us; indeed, while greater clarity can emerge as the years and decades pass, this remains a 'work in progress' right up to the moment of death. And for most philosophers of education, it is not as if there is any *one* line of thought to which we are devoted. Ideas evolve and change, as we encounter and engage the work of others, as we teach and learn from students and as we negotiate the rigours of life beyond the academy. But regardless of what, when, why and for whom one writes, there remains in all such efforts at least some trace of the drive to preserve something of ourselves.

---

8   See further, Roberts (2022).
9   Arendt (1998) speaks of the potential we have as mortals to produce things – our 'works and deeds and words' – that deserve to be 'at home in everlastingness' (p. 19).

We want to leave something behind that speaks to 'us': to what we stand for, to what matters most to us.

In a more abstract sense, and building on the observations above, we might say that education works against death in its favouring of preservation and continuity. We preserve what we know, or think we know, in books and articles. We create repositories of knowledge in physical and electronic libraries. We house creative works in galleries and museums. There is a continuous passing on of knowledge from one generation to the next. Some fields of study may be only a few decades old, but others stretch back centuries, linking teachers, students and their subject matter across the ages. Even if there are fallow periods in the history of a discipline, and even if what counts as legitimate knowledge or rigorous research in a particular domain of study may change over time, the overall tendency to 'hold on' to what we know remains. This is evident in other ways. If education is, in one way or another, a *critical* endeavour, with an emphasis on the asking of questions and the posing of problems, it can rouse us from sleep and work against the propensity to forget.[10] These possibilities are consistent with the role Unamuno assumed, through his writing, as a teacher. In a pedagogical sense, Unamuno wanted, more than anything else, to *keep us awake*. He saw sleep as a step towards death, and his strongest impulse was to resist this – to stay alert, alive and aware. A teacher who takes Unamuno as a guide will want to not only stimulate reflection but actively create discomfort among learners. Unamuno (1972) talks of avoiding lulling others to sleep by arousing in them the 'anguish and torment of spirit' that is fundamental to the human condition (p. 306). This is an approach to education that does not allow us to ever fully relax. Education, conceived in these terms, is a form of agitation – a disruptive, destabilising process. We end up living in a kind of permanent educational insomnia.

There is much that can be questioned in this account. For some learners, the dramatic 'awakening' promoted by Unamuno could be counterproductive, alienating them from their teachers and deterring them from further reflection and investigation. Sometimes a gentler, more subtle and gradual stirring

---

10 'Remembering' can be seen as important in education from a number of other perspectives. We might speak, for instance, of 'memory work' as an ethical commitment to acknowledge and respond to past injustices (cf. Ricoeur, 2006). It is also possible to see learning itself as fundamentally a process of recollection. This view was advanced by Plato (1949, 1974) and was premised on the notion that as beings with immortal souls, we can, with appropriate pedagogical prompting, recollect or recover what we already knew from previous lives.

of the critical senses is necessary. Wakefulness can be exhausting, and rest is also needed. 'Switching off' completely may not be possible, for once a critical orientation toward the world has been formed, there is no going back. We may deny that questions are there, or self-consciously avoid problematising complex situations, but the voice of critical reason keeps prodding away at us in the background. That being so, we can nevertheless speak of periods of 'active recovery', where the inner tensions to which Unamuno refers are moderated by other activities (e.g. meditation, or exercise, or service to our communities).[11] We can experience the same troubling thoughts and emotions but respond to them in different ways.[12] It is possible to be distressed or disturbed – even in despair – without living in a state of constant agitation. We can come to accept that there will be much that we *cannot* accept – cannot ignore, cannot support – in the way the world works. We can remain calm while dealing with stressful situations, including those we create for ourselves in pondering ethical dilemmas. Indeed, the tensions to which Unamuno refers can themselves become the object of patient, loving attention, and this can be an educative process. First, however, we must learn to slow down, to listen, to watch and to wait. We must avoid the temptation to impose ourselves and our categories for understanding too quickly on the object of our attention. Developing our capacity for educative attention requires patience and persistence, especially when facing uncomfortable truths. The benefits of our work in cultivating this capacity may not be felt immediately but will often be experienced later in life, sometimes in areas of human endeavour seemingly disconnected from those in which the original effort of attention was applied.[13]

In *The Tragic Sense of Life*, Unamuno maintains that suffering is preferable to the prospect of nothingness, for in suffering there is still life; to exist in pain, he insists, is better than not existing at all. We might wonder, however, just how far he would take this logic. Unamuno confesses that he was never convinced by descriptions of eternal punishment in hell; for him, nothingness is itself the most hellish thing one could imagine (p. 49). But this is hardly convincing.[14] It is not difficult to imagine situations where pain and suffering are so great, so severe and sustained, that nothingness would seem preferable. Unamuno holds on to the hope of immortality, free of the burden of believing that a 'fire and brimstone'

---

11 These points are developed more fully in Roberts and Saeverot (2018, Chapter 4).
12 See further, Jackson (2022) and Roberts (2016).
13 The notion of attention articulated here draws on Murdoch (2001) and Weil (1997, 2001).
14 This aspect of Unamuno's work is analysed in more detail in Roberts et al. (2023).

version of hell awaits him. He says little, however, about what he expects to find should he survive beyond death. He is reluctant to speculate at length on the possibilities, preferring instead to sustain a state of uncertainty. He is clear though that if he is to endure, he would want to do so as he is, continuing to live as if in his present life. But this too raises important ethical and educational questions. Living on endlessly, whether this is without death or after death, could denude many of our usual activities of their significance. Without the finitude imposed by death, our sense of having to commit, to take risks, to set priorities, could diminish. With unlimited time in front of us, why, we might ask ourselves, should we struggle to achieve anything? Even the most precious connections we have – to loved ones – could begin to lose their value, with relationships developing and disappearing, one after the other, in a life that stretches on interminably. These possibilities are highlighted in Simone de Beauvoir's (1992) novel, *All Men Are Mortal*.

Be Careful What You Wish For

The initial focus of the narrative in *All Men Are Mortal* is on the character Regina, who, despite a successful acting career, remains restless and dissatisfied with her life. One day she meets a stranger, Raymond Fosca, who reveals a secret to her: he is immortal. He tells her that he was born in 1279, in Carmona, Italy. Raised by his father and educated by monks, he marries, has a son and rises to prominence in his part of the world. Offered an elixir of immortality by a beggar, and fuelled by an ambition to achieve more for himself and for Carmona, he drinks the potion and thereafter cannot die. His skills as a leader allow Carmona to escape some of the worst effects of the weather, avoiding the ravages of the famine faced by others, but disease and death follow. With his own family all gone, he sees himself as beholden to no one, as free but forever alone. He witnesses the same patterns of human behaviour repeating themselves endlessly, with periods of peace and prosperity followed by conflict and hardship. He travels the world, forms new friendships and relationships, makes himself wealthy and eventually finds his way to Paris. He becomes familiar with many of the city's attractions but cannot experience fulfilment in anything. He meets a woman, Marianne, who, in her earnest commitment to social causes, provides a sharp contrast with his cynicism and weariness. He allows himself to fall in love again, but when Marianne discovers his secret, a rift develops between them. This heals over time, but as Marianne sees her own death approaching, she realises that she too, like the other women in

Fosca's life, will eventually be forgotten. Fosca lives on, through an epidemic, the rise of a Republican movement and the continuing cycle of birth, suffering and death. He falls asleep for sixty years, waking to find the world little changed, and is placed in an asylum. Regina, who has been listening to this story being told, watches Fosca disappear down the road and is left, in despair, to contemplate her own fate. The novel closes with her letting out a scream.

Both Regina and Fosca exhibit many of the human tendencies identified by Unamuno. Regina has a longing to distinguish herself among her peers, to create something through her work that will have lasting significance and value. For outsiders looking in, she may seem to have it all, but she is far from content. She wants more from her relationships with others, more from her surroundings and more from herself. She finds that she cannot breeze nonchalantly through life, but instead experiences the tensions associated with the 'disease' that is reflective consciousness. Fosca too eagerly pursues the prospect of immortality, only to find, having attained it, that he does not want it. Before he begins telling his story to Regina, he warns her that immortality is a curse. At various points in his long existence, he commits himself fully to others, experiencing both the joy that can go with this and the suffering to which Unamuno refers, but as time goes by, he finds himself forgetting even those who were closest to him. In some cases, he works hard to resist this, but he has only limited success in doing so. With the passing of years, he finds it increasingly difficult to retain his memory of the faces, the gestures, the words, of loved ones. Fosca endures endlessly, yet he does not feel alive. Having all the time in the world to pursue his interests reduces rather than enhances the sense of satisfaction he feels in completing a project or achieving a goal. Others can risk it all for something, or someone, they believe in; Fosca cannot. For Fosca, unlimited time sets its own limits.[15] His life lacks the structure and form that would enable him to *form himself*. He lives on a flat plane of existence, the long march of decades and centuries tending to level out the contours, the peaks and troughs, characteristic of other lives. He can build relationships with others, but he cannot connect with them in a lasting way. He is a stranger in the world.

Unamuno, in his writing and his conduct, provided a robust critique of indifference. He cared, deeply and passionately, about the ideas he explored and the people who were close to him. Fosca finds that in living on and on,

---

15 Much depends here on how we understand time. For more on different conceptions of time, and the role of education in shaping them, see Mikulan and Sinclair (2023).

a certain indifference is difficult to avoid. In his observations of others, and his understanding of himself, there are, as the centuries pass, fewer and fewer surprises. People struggle and strive, for love, power, happiness or a sense of purpose in their lives, and then they die. At times, Fosca comes to believe that nothing really matters – at least not for him, and perhaps not for others as well. Fosca's situation differs from many where the idea of immortality is considered: in the novel, he *has never died*, here on Earth, whereas in most discussions of immortality, the question is considered in relation to what happens after our physical death. For Unamuno, as we have seen, it was precisely the continuation of life as if he has never died – that is, of his present existence – that he wanted. For others, this may not be the case: there may be an anticipation of something better as the transition is made from death into a heavenly realm. For yet others, it may not be eternal life that is wanted, either without death or after it, but simply a *longer* life. It is an interesting educational exercise to contemplate the prospect of living for, say, 200 or 500 or 1000 years. Applied on a global scale, with the opportunity to lengthen the lifespan open to all, such a scenario could pose difficult ethical questions and create serious practical problems. Still, there is value in pondering what we might truly want – for ourselves and for others – if our any wish could be granted. With recent developments in science, medicine and technology, hypothetical possibilities are now being investigated as future realities.

Beauvoir's fictional character Fosca comes to regret his decision to drink the elixir of immortality, but the desire to live on seems to be as strong as ever in the contemporary world. A number of organisations, some spearheaded by scientists, others underpinned by corporate interests, have been established with the aim of extending or reviving biological life. Some see the prevention of telomere shortening as our best prospect in reducing or eliminating the effects of ageing; others hold on to the hope offered by cryogenic technologies or envisage a time when cells might be repaired through nanotechnology or parts of the body might be replaced through cloning (Peters, 2021). As Peters observes, however, '[i]f we ever achieve biological immortality, we may not come to see it as entirely desirable. Over a near infinite lifespan after years of boredom we might feel blessed to accept a graceful death' (p. 562). The prospect of finding life less engaging as time stretches out interminably is certainly problematic, as Fosca discovers in Beauvoir's novel. But another more worrying possibility must also be considered. As we live on, we carry with us not just memories of pleasurable experiences but also those associated with upsetting situations and encounters. Feelings of fear, anger, disappointment and sadness can linger for a lifetime. Traumatic events and circumstances can leave deep scars that never heal. We may have to endure sustained periods of intense discomfort and pain.[16] The weight of these accumulated burdens, carved into our continuing individual consciousnesses, could, as decades or centuries pass, become too difficult to bear. Unamuno's expressed preference for suffering over non-existence was based on just the memories gathered over his life to that point. Had he endured for centuries or millennia, with layer upon layer of suffering built up over time, it is conceivable that he may have changed his position. We do not know, and nor could he. What we can recognise and respect is the role his passionate will to live played in sustaining him – but also troubling him – in the existence he did have.

The idea of an extended or eternal life raises important questions about the significance of memory, and of forgetting, in shaping who and what we are. Some people are fortified by a belief that after they die, they will dwell forever in a paradise, surrounded by love, beauty and goodness. They may be of the view that if we enter this realm, we shed the burdens of our earthly existence, leaving behind all that was unpleasant, including painful memories. But who are 'we' if this is the case? 'We' are not who we were; we become partial renditions of ourselves. If we can rid ourselves of all that is distressing in what we recollect of our past, we lose much that makes us what we are. *Something* may endure, but it is no longer us – or, at least, not us in the fullest sense possible. And if there are others in this paradise with us – people who may, for instance, have been precious to us before they died – they too, if they have undergone the same process of having painful memories wiped from their consciousnesses, will be but shadows of their former selves. Another possibility is that, with the fresh perspective granted to us in an afterlife, painful memories are transformed rather than eliminated.[17] We may retain a vivid sense of what has hurt us in the past, but be able to come to terms with this – to view

---

16 Nietzsche (1989) maintains that 'only that which never ceases to *hurt* stays in the memory'; if 'something is to stay in the memory it must be burned in' (p. 61). He sees forgetting as an active and positive form of repression. Active forgetfulness is 'like a doorkeeper, a preserver of psychic order, repose, and etiquette'; without forgetfulness, 'there could be no happiness, nor cheerfulness, no hope, no pride, no *present*' (p. 58). See also Nietzsche (1997) and Draz (2018).

17 As Ricoeur (2006) points out, if 'events are ineradicable – if one cannot undo what is done or make what has happened not happen – on the other hand, the *meaning* of what has happened is not fixed once and for all' (pp. 14–15). Ricoeur argues that 'unhappy memory, touched by the spirit of forgiveness, is open to transformation in time' (Duffy, 2012, p. 83). If 'hurt memories are to be transformed then we have to be able to consider from a distance,

it through different eyes, guided, perhaps, by others who have done likewise. But this prospect poses its own problems, for at a certain point, suffering radically reconfigured is no longer suffering at all – and for Unamuno, as for other thinkers examined in this book, this would mean that an essential element in our formation and continuation as distinctive individual beings would have been lost.

Other ways of living on, in digital form, have also been considered. A certain kind of immortality might be attained, for example, via the uploading of some representation of our consciousnesses to a computer. We might imagine a situation where our loved ones could communicate with us in this form, after we have gone, speaking to a digital device (or typing instructions, or clicking on a mouse button) and having it respond as we might have while still alive. A detailed database of facts about our lives might be entered into a programme, along with some of our known likes and dislikes, to ensure accuracy and consistency in the answers given to questions. We might 'train' the system to mimic our manner of speaking, even perhaps to share our sense of humour. 'Afterlife' versions of ourselves might also be projected via holograms or reconstructed from prerecorded video footage. But, again, questions can be asked about what would remain of 'us' under such scenarios.[18] As human beings, we form our identities with bodies, located in physical spaces, through our interactions with others and the world. We cannot, in any helpful holistic sense, be adequately contained in a digital file, captured in an online profile or (re)generated by an algorithm. As Stokes (2012) puts it, 'if asked whether such a form of online posthumous persistence would be somewhat as good as surviving death, we might instead reply that it's not even meaningfully *comparable* to survival' (p. 371). This point would hold even if we could be transferred to a new entity with a physical form that resembled our own – a synthetic copy of ourselves, with a digital 'brain' – for it would remain just that: a *copy*, a simulation. We would, in a sense, be cheating both ourselves and those dearest to us who do not want to let us go.

While efforts to become immortal are unlikely to cease any time soon, it is also important to protect the right to *not* continue in certain forms. There is already a substantial problem in dealing with digital remains (e.g. social

---

the stage upon which memories of the past are invited to make an appearance, if we are to truly claim them as our own, in order to be unbound from them eventually' (p. 83).

18 For a range of perspectives on death and continuity in the digital age, see Harbinja (2023); Lagerkvist (2015); Lehner (2019); Meese et al. (2015); Öhman and Floridi (2017) and Stokes (2012, 2015a).

media accounts for dead people), but ethical questions also need to be posed in relation to other commonly accepted twenty-first century practices. We live increasingly 'recorded' lives. In using cell phones, a detailed map of where we go, when and with whom can emerge. We leave traces of ourselves – our interests and preferences – every time we browse the Internet. Our movements – on city streets, at airports and in shops, restaurants, hospitals, courts, police stations and educational institutions – are captured on video by surveillance cameras. The monitoring of human activity in this way will often be justified on the basis that it is necessary for security reasons or perhaps to protect others who may be vulnerable. It might be argued that we tacitly consent to these measures, to a greater or lesser extent, because they tend to be applied in settings and situations that could theoretically be avoided. And many add to the impression that an ever-expanding range of recorded activities is desirable by posting photographs and videos of themselves to online sites. But attitudes are often too casual in dealing with these developments. We can find ourselves preserved in digital form without our knowledge, let alone our explicit consent. This can occur in our educational activities, with, for example, class recordings or seminars or conference addresses being filmed and posted online without our permission. It is not just privacy that is at stake here (though that is of vital importance), but also the integrity of our educational encounters. To gather together, as teachers and students in a classroom, or as colleagues at a conference, is to participate in a distinctive educational event – one that defies duplication and that cannot be fully understood or appreciated beyond the context in which it takes place.

We might say, then, that students, teachers and citizens have a right to determine, as far as this is possible, what of themselves is preserved (and in that sense, rendered immortal). But from an educational perspective we can go further than this. As Simone Weil (2002) points out, for every right it is possible to identify a corresponding obligation, and this idea is relevant when considering the consequences of our digital archiving activities. As the range of surveillance mechanisms in place in contemporary societies continues to increase and to morph into more subtle and sophisticated forms, the need for educational work in this domain becomes more pressing. Thus, while we can advance an ethical principle that we have an obligation to consider others before photographing, filming or recording them, more is required of us. There is an educational task in drawing attention to the range of tracking and monitoring systems currently employed or under consideration and in discussing and debating them with students and colleagues. We can also attempt to step back a little from 'business as usual' and ask *why* we wish to preserve – and share – so many different elements of our lives, and other lives, in recorded form. Drawing on Unamuno, we might say that these developments represent an expression of our deep desire, often unrecognised, to live on. But this is perhaps not a complete explanation. We also need to consider, for instance, how multinational corporations stand to gain by tracking our activities and encouraging citizens to aid them in this process (e.g. through creating comprehensive digital profiles of themselves). Wants, preferences and habits do not emerge from nowhere; they are, of course, influenced and shaped by the social and economic structures of our time. There is educational work to do in not only getting to grips with the politics of digital preservation and continuation but also in setting recent technological developments in their broader historical contexts.

Making Death Matter

Thus far, the focus has been mainly on personal immortality. We have seen that Unamuno had a deep longing to live on and that he believed the drive to do so was also present in others. Questions have been raised about the desirability of immortality, both in the form envisaged by Unamuno and in a range of other ways. We can, the discussion to this point has indicated, both seek immortality for ourselves and have it created for us by others. But we can also consider the idea of another type of 'afterlife': this is the world we anticipate will continue, here on Earth, after we have died (Scheffler, 2013). Our first thoughts when contemplating the afterlife in this sense will often be with those nearest and dearest to us. We want the people we love to have good lives after we have gone. Our musings on these matters may extend beyond these immediate concerns to the fate of other people, other species and the planet. As Cicero (2017) noted, 'while death presents a daily threat because of the uncertainties of chance, and while it can never be far away because of the shortness of life, it does not deter the wise man from taking thought for his country and his loved ones for all time' (p. 38). We can also think about those who have died, or may well die, 'before their time' as a result of social injustices. We can ponder the prioritising of some lives, human and non-human, over others. There is no neutral ground to stand on in these matters, and difficult decisions often need to be made. In seeking to preserve native birds and animals, for instance, other introduced predator species sometimes have to be killed. If we are to understand death, we need to examine the complex web of connections and relationships that structure human and non-human lives. A person's death always involves others, directly or indirectly, in the manner through which the death occurs, in the emotional consequences of the death and in the rites enacted to honour the deceased, among other ways. A longing to live on after death will also often be heavily influenced by a strong desire to rejoin loved ones who have already passed away.

And yet, for each of us, death and the process of dying must also be experienced individually. We are shaped by the social, political and cultural conditions of our time and place, but we cannot be reduced to those formative factors. There is, for human beings at least, always something more to 'us' – as existing individuals in the Kierkegaardian sense – than the sum of our relationships, influences and connections.[19] The same principle applies to the idea of immortality: 'A person composed of nothing but his social relations and qualifications simply would not exist if he passed into an afterlife in which those relationships no longer held; there is nothing that could pass into the afterlife and *still be him*' (Stokes, 2015b, p. 193). Inasmuch as we are all subject to it, death is universal. As a shared reality, death creates an invisible bond between us; a connecting thread, thin though it may be, that links all living creatures to each other. But an encounter with death will always be singular. From an educational perspective, then, any attempt to provide clear guidelines for learning to die – rules or procedures or practices that will apply in exactly the same way for all people, in all circumstances, at all times – will fall short of what is needed. That does not mean we cannot ponder some of the possibilities open to us. Indeed, the very act of posing and responding to these questions – of reflecting on death, dying and immortality – is itself important from an educational point of view. We need not obsess over death in quite the same manner as Unamuno, but we can make it much more central to our everyday conscious activities. Aurelius (2011) advised us to let 'every action, word, and thought be those of one who could depart from life at any moment' (p. 12). And Montaigne (1991), echoing the Stoic view, argued that by allowing the prospect of death to inhabit our consciousness we can loosen its grip over us. By making death part of life, recognising that in living we are also dying, we can better prepare ourselves for the end when it comes.[20]

---

19 Kierkegaard's position on the existing individual is developed in detail in *Concluding Unscientific Postscript* (Kierkegaard, 2009).
20 Heidegger (1996) sees death as a 'phenomenon of life' and argues that a 'this-worldly, ontological interpretation of death comes before any ontic, other-worldly speculation' (pp. 229–230). For a Heideggerian perspective on death and education, see Yun (2011).

Building on these ideas, we can say that it is not just a matter of learning *about* death but also *from* it and *with* it. We might even conceive of death as a *teacher*. We are all, each in our own distinctive ways, students of death. Death can be seen as a kind of companion, accompanying us throughout our lives, always promising to appear but remaining forever hidden, withdrawn, silent. Death exerts a powerful influence over us – over what we think and feel and do – without 'itself' doing anything. It is always 'there' for us, at some point in the future (but at an exact moment we cannot ordinarily predict), and we are always working towards it. Death in this sense provides the ultimate end – in two senses of that word – for all education. And yet, death itself, for the existing individual, is unknowable and unreachable. We can experience the process of dying – and the whole of life can be seen as exactly that – but we cannot say, in precise terms, what it means to die. For Unamuno, it is the uncertainty over what happens to us *after* we die that provides hope, but we do not know what it 'is' to die. Hence, if we are to see death as a teacher, this is a pedagogue who is always somewhat out of reach. But the process of seeking to grasp what is being offered by death can itself be educative. In facing the mystery that is death, our posture should be one of humility and openness. Humility need not be produced by fear, and we need not feel absolute terror in the face of death. We can be humble in recognition of the dominion death has over us all – its reach and power. But humility can be partnered with openness in wanting to learn with and from this mysterious teacher. By remaining hidden, while all the while ushering us forwards, death can foster a certain curiosity and prompt us to ask questions, probe further and investigate.

We are here on Earth to learn, and if there is anything worthy of a commitment to *lifelong* learning, it is death. For Unamuno (1972), it is 'ceaseless learning', not 'knowing', to which we should become committed (p. 250). Once we think we know something, we can put it to one side, believing our work is done. Knowledge can become static, lifeless, 'dead' to us. Seeking to learn, in the manner envisaged by Unamuno, implies exploration, discovery, movement. If death – that is, our individual death, not the deaths of others or our own process of *dying* – can never be known, 'learning to die' is always a kind of provisional preparation. We are preparing for a moment that, for us as existing individuals, never comes. This holds true irrespective of our views on what comes 'after' death. Unamuno was horrified by the prospect of nothingness, but he could not explain what this is. Indeed, as he saw it, no one could: consciousness, he argued, cannot comprehend its own non-existence. If we believe something persists beyond biological death, we likewise cannot know, definitively, what that 'something' is. We often speak of death as one of the few certainties in life. But while we may be certain *that* we die, almost everything else we might say about death remains *un*certain. This suggests that a key element of the process of learning to die might be learning to live with uncertainty prior to death. Death, through its unknowability, invites inquiry, encouraging us to keep learning throughout life, while also refusing to provide easy answers. Learning to live with uncertainty means more than grudgingly putting up with it, wishing we could know for sure. Uncertainty also becomes more than a 'coping mechanism' for dealing with the fear of death. We live *in* and *through* uncertainty, mindful of its dangers when taken to extremes, while also relishing its liberating potential in stimulating a lifelong interest in learning.

Cultivating and retaining a sense of mystery – being open to limits in our understanding of reality, and of ourselves – can play an important part in our educational formation. This is seldom recognised in our formal systems of education, particularly in the West, where the emphasis is on knowing and knowledge, rather than on deepening our appreciation of the unknowable (Mika, 2015). As noted near the start of this book, we live in a world of exaggerated certainties, where doubt is often construed as a weakness. In acknowledging that there are some things that may never be known, we can begin to break down these prejudices and come to see uncertainty as a highly desirable trait. For Unamuno, as we have seen, it is not merely a matter of learning to live with uncertainty but of actively embracing it. Uncertainty provides hope, and hope is necessary in going on. Being uncertain need not mean we are unable to get anything done. We can still make decisions and take action while remaining uncertain; we may simply be more inclined (than those who appear to brook no doubt) to consider carefully how to act in a given situation. We may reflect at greater length on what is at stake in the decisions we make and on the possible consequences of the actions we take. In negotiating many of practical problems we face in daily life, it is seldom a simple matter of being either 'certain' or 'uncertain'. We may be more certain about some things than others. Our sense of what we are more or less certain about can shift over time and will often be influenced by the ideas to which we become exposed and the people with whom we come into contact. Valuing uncertainty need not mean jumping about from one position to the next. There can, across a long life committed to learning, be a strong sense of thematic unity – of coherence and continuity – in the questions addressed and the avenues through which answers are pursued. But thinking about death and (un)certainty in this way suggests an ongoing educational process, a willingness, throughout the lifespan, to examine past and present beliefs and practices and an openness to the prospect of change.[21]

Conclusion

Unamuno may have been unusual in the intensity of his desire to live on, but his work provides an important reminder of how significant death can be in shaping what we think, feel and do. Fosca, in Beauvoir's *All Men Are Mortal*, found that immortality led him toward a certain indifference in relation to life. Yet, crucially, he was not indifferent in his views on death. Just as Unamuno longed for eternal life, Fosca longed for death. Fosca may not have had to endure the same consequences as other citizens in all activities – he could not die in fighting on the battlefield, for instance – but his immortality did not shield him from all forms of pain. He suffered in and through love, and he experienced the despair of loneliness as a stranger in the world. Death mattered for Fosca, as it should for all committed to the task of education. We should, this chapter has suggested, come to *care* about death: our own death and the deaths of others.

We can bring death 'out of the closet' and discuss it more openly in educational settings, but caution is needed in moving in this direction. Consideration needs to be given to the cultural and religious backgrounds of students and to the distress that can be experienced by those who remember lost loved ones.[22] The age of those being taught also needs to be taken into account. Young children can and do ask thoughtful and probing questions about death and dying, but care must be taken to avoid imposing our views as adults on them. At higher levels in the education system, we might encourage students to read widely on death, not just as a subject for theoretical and empirical study but also as a theme explored in literature, film, theatre and the other arts. We can address questions relating to death, dying and (im)mortality in our written work as philosophers of education. Most of all, we can, with humility, openness and curiosity, allow death to *teach us*, setting out on an educational journey that may be unsettling, uncertain and difficult but ultimately worthwhile.

---

21 For more on the nature and place of uncertainty in education, see Roberts (2021).
22 Some students may, for example, come from backgrounds where death is treated as a 'taboo' subject, not to be discussed for 'fear of invoking bad luck' (Hsu et al., 2009, p. 154).

References

Affifi, R. & Christie, B. (2019). Facing loss: Pedagogy of death. *Environmental Education Research*, 25(8), 1143–1157.

Arcilla, R. V. (1997). Education of the undead? In S. Laird (Ed.), *Philosophy of Education 1997* (pp. 449–451). Philosophy of Education Society.

Arendt, H. (1998). *The human condition* (2nd edition). University of Chicago Press.

Aurelius, M. (2011). *Meditations* (R. Hard, Trans.). Oxford University Press.

Beauvoir, S. de (1992). *All men are mortal* (L. M. Friedman, Trans.). W. W. Norton.

Bertoldo, J. C. (2023). Thinking *with* death: An educational proposition in the interest of publicness. In T. Wilson (Ed.), *Philosophy of Education 2023* (pp. 19–33). Philosophy of Education Society.

Blacker, D. (1998). Education as immortality: Toward the rehabilitation of an ideal. *Religious Education*, 93, 8–28.

Cicero (2017). *On life and death* (J. Davie, Trans.). Oxford University Press.

Dahlbeck, J. (2015). Educating for immortality: Spinoza and the pedagogy of gradual existence. *Journal of Philosophy of Education*, 49(3), 347–365.

Dhillon, P. (1997). Teaching to death. In S. Laird (Ed.), *Philosophy of Education 1997* (pp. 452–455). Philosophy of Education Society.

Draz, M. (2018). Burning it in: Nietzsche, gender, and externalized memory. *Feminist Philosophy Quarterly*, 4(2), 1–21.

Duffy, M. (2012). *Paul Ricoeur's pedagogy of pardon: A narrative theory of memory and forgetting*. Bloomsbury.

Evans, J. E. (2013). *Miguel de Unamuno's quest for faith: A Kierkegaardian understanding of Unamuno's struggle to believe*. Pickwick Publications.

Hadot, P. (1995). *Philosophy as a way of life*. (M. Chase, Trans.). Blackwell.

Harbinja, E. (2023). *Digital death, digital assets and post-mortem privacy*. Edinburgh University Press.

Heidegger, M. (1996). *Being and time* (J. Stambaugh, Trans.). State University of New York Press.

Herrán Gascón, A. de la, Rodríguez Herrero, P. & Miguel Yubero, V. de (2024). Beyond death education? A study of its epistemological traditions [¿Más allá de la death education? Un estudio sobre sus tradiciones epistemológicas]. *Teoría de la Educación. Revista Interuniversitaria*, 36(1), 183–204.

Hsu, C-Y., O'Connor, M. & Lee, S. (2009). Understandings of death and dying for people of Chinese origin. *Death Studies*, 33(2), 153–174.

Jackson, L. (2022). *Beyond virtue: The politics of educating emotions*. Cambridge University Press.

Johansson, V. (2022). Sámi children as thought herders: Philosophy of death and storytelling as radical hope in early childhood education. *Policy Futures in Education*, 20(3), 316–331.

Kierkegaard, S. (2009). *Concluding unscientific postscript* (A. Hannay, Trans.). Cambridge University Press.

Lagerkvist, A. (2015). The netlore of the infinite: Death (and beyond) in the digital memory ecology. *New Review of Hypermedia and Multimedia*, 21(1–2), 185–195.

Lehner, N. (2019). The work of the digital undead: Digital capitalism and the suspension of communicative death. *Continuum, 33*(4), 475–488.

Lucretius (1999). *On the nature of the universe* (R. Melville, Trans.). Oxford University Press.

Meese, J., Nansen, B., Kohn, T., Arnold, M. & Gibbs, M. (2015). Posthumous personhood and the affordances of digital media. *Mortality, 20*(4), 408–420.

Mika, C. (2015). Counter-colonial and philosophical claims: An indigenous observation of Western philosophy. *Educational Philosophy and Theory, 47*(11), 1136–1142.

Mikulan, P. & Sinclair, N. (2023). *Time and education: Time pedagogy against oppression*. Bloomsbury.

Montaigne, M. de (1991). *The complete essays* (M. A. Screech, Trans.). Penguin.

Murdoch, I. (2001). *The sovereignty of good*. Routledge.

Neiman, A. M. (1997). Teaching and eternal life: The love of learning and desire for God. In S. Laird (Ed.), *Philosophy of Education 1997* (pp. 456–460). Philosophy of Education Society.

Nietzsche, F. (1989). *On the genealogy of morals* and *Ecce homo* (W. Kaufmann, Trans.). Vintage.

Nietzsche, F. (1997). *Untimely meditations* (R. J. Hollingdale, Trans., D. Breazeale, Ed.). Cambridge University Press.

Öhman, C. J. & Floridi, L. (2017). The political economy of death in the age of information: A critical approach to the digital afterlife industry. *Minds and Machines, 27*, 639–662.

Peters, M. A. (2021). Against death. Longevity forever! *Educational Philosophy and Theory, 53*(6), 559–562.

Plato. (1949). The Meno (F. Sydenham, Trans.). In Plato, *Five dialogues* (pp. 82–132). Everyman's Library.

Plato. (1974). *The Republic* (H. D. P. Lee, Trans.). Penguin.

Plato (2003). *The last days of Socrates* (H. Tredennick & H. Tarrant, Trans.). Penguin.

Puolimatka, T. & Solasaari, U. (2006). Education for death. *Educational Philosophy and Theory, 38*, 201–214.

Ricoeur, P. (2006). Memory-forgetting-history. In J. Rüsen (Ed.), *Meaning and representation in history* (pp. 9–19). Berghahn Books.

Roberts, P. (2012). *From West to East and back again: An educational reading of Hermann Hesse's later work*. Sense Publishers.

Roberts, P. (2016). *Happiness, hope, and despair: Rethinking the role of education*. Peter Lang.

Roberts, P. (2021). More than measurement: Education, uncertainty and existence. In P. Howard, T. Saevi, A. Foran & G. Biesta (Eds.), *Phenomenology and educational theory in conversation: Back to education itself* (pp. 63–74). Routledge.

Roberts, P. (2022). *Performativity, politics and education: From policy to philosophy*. Brill.

Roberts, P. & Saeverot, H. (2018). *Education and the limits of reason: Reading Dostoevsky, Tolstoy and Nabokov*. Routledge.

Roberts, P., Webster, R. S. & Quay, J. (2023). *Philosophy, death and education*. Peter Lang.

Savin-Baden, M. (2019). Postdigital afterlife? *Postdigital Science and Education, 1*, 303–306.

Scheffler, S. (2013). *Death and the afterlife* (N. Kolodny, Ed.). New York: Oxford University Press.

Schwieler, E. (2022). *Aporias of translation: Literature, philosophy, education*. Springer.

Seneca (2007). *Dialogues and essays* (J. Davie, Trans.). Oxford University Press.

Shim, S. (2020). The existential meaning of death and reconsidering death education through the perspectives of Kierkegaard and Heidegger. *Educational Philosophy and Theory, 52*(9), 973–985.

Smeyers, P., Smith, R. & Standish, P. (2007). *The therapy of education: Philosophy, happiness and personal growth*. Palgrave Macmillan.

Stokes, P. (2012). Ghosts in the machine: Do the dead live on in Facebook? *Philosophy and Technology, 25,* 363–379.

Stokes, P. (2015a). Deletion as second death: The moral status of digital remains. *Ethics and Information Technology, 17,* 237–248.

Stokes, P. (2015b). *The naked self: Kierkegaard and personal identity*. Oxford University Press.

Unamuno, M. de (1972). *The tragic sense of life in men and nations* (A. Kerrigan, Trans.). Princeton University Press.

Unamuno, M. de (1996). *Abel Sanchez and other stories* (A. Kerrigan, Trans.). Regnery Publishing.

van Kessel, C. & Burke, K. (2018). Teaching as an immortality project: Positing weakness in response to terror. *Journal of Philosophy of Education, 52*(2), 216–229.

Weil, S. (1997). *Gravity and grace* (A. Wills, Trans.). Bison Books.

Weil, S. (2001). *Waiting for God* (E. Craufurd, Trans.). Perennial Classics.

Weil, S. (2002). *The need for roots* (A. Wills, Trans.). Routledge.

Yun, S. (2011). Can death be taught? Finding meaning, mortality, and culture. In N. Saito (Ed.), *Finding meaning, cultures across borders: International dialogue between philosophy and psychology* (pp. 87–94). Proceedings of the 4th International Symposium between the Graduate School of Education, Kyoto University (Japan), and the Institute of Education, University of London (UK).

CREDITS

The author and publisher gratefully acknowledge permission to reproduce material from the following sources.

One paragraph in the Introduction draws, in part, on Roberts, P. (2020). Less certain but no less committed: Paulo Freire and Simone de Beauvoir on ethics and education. In J.D. Kirylo (Ed.), *Reinventing* Pedagogy of the Oppressed: *Contemporary critical perspectives* (pp. 135–146). Bloomsbury. By permission of Bloomsbury Academic, an imprint of Bloomsbury Publishing Plc.

Chapter 3 was initially published as Roberts, P. (2023). Education and the ethics of attention: The work of Simone Weil. *British Journal of Educational Studies*, 71(3), 267–284. Copyright © 2022 Society for Educational Studies, reprinted by permission of Informa UK Limited, trading as Taylor & Francis Group, www.tandfonline.com, on behalf of the Society for Educational Studies.

Chapter 4 is a substantially expanded version of Roberts, P. (2024). The stranger as teacher. In J. Baldacchino & H. Saeverot (Eds.), *The Bloomsbury handbook of Continental philosophy of education* (pp. 389–399). Bloomsbury Academic. By permission of Bloomsbury Academic, an imprint of Bloomsbury Publishing Plc.

INDEX

Absorption 44–46
All Men Are Mortal 117–119, 127
Ambiguity 4
Art 2, 6, 16, 18–19, 27, 29, 35–36, 40, 45, 57–58, 70, 76–77, 90, 97
Attention 7, 9, 20, 26, 45, 55, 74–81, 98, 116
Aurelius 124
Awakening 7, 20, 33, 87, 113, 115

Barreto, Lima 96
Beauty 19, 24, 27, 36, 45–47, 76–79, 120
Beauvoir, Simone de 3, 10, 67, 70, 88, 92, 117–119, 127

Calmness 26, 45, 71, 103
Camus, Albert 35, 70, 88, 92
Certainty 3, 12, 60, 126–127
Cervantes, Miguel de 5, 7, 10, 86, 90–98, 103
Children 17–18, 25, 33, 50–51, 54, 74–76, 99, 112, 127
Christianity 50, 68–70, 76
Cicero 123
Classroom 2–3, 87–88, 98–102, 122
Conspiracy mindset 56

Contemplation 7, 9, 44–47, 101
Continuity 115, 121, 126
Conversation 7, 10, 49, 53, 56, 96, 100–101, 108
Curriculum 3–4, 7, 77
Curiosity 2, 6, 34, 49, 125, 127

Darkness 5–6, 31
Death 8, 10–12, 18, 22–24, 27–31, 44, 68, 93–94, 96, 107–127
Decreation 2, 9, 35, 66, 70–71, 74–75, 79
Despair 2, 4–6, 11–12, 16–17, 20, 23–24, 26–36, 44, 52–53, 67, 73, 75, 80, 89, 91, 93, 97, 111–113, 116, 118, 127
Dienstag, Joshua 5, 10, 94–96
Discomfort 3, 5, 24, 89, 97, 115, 120
Don Quixote 86, 90–102
Dostoevsky, Fyodor 35, 70, 78, 92
Dread 46

Edges 4, 12
Elitism 52
Epicurus 10, 108
Existence 2, 4, 6, 8–9, 17, 26–28, 31–34, 44, 60, 70, 89, 92–93, 108, 112, 118–120, 125

INDEX

Experience 2, 4–6, 8, 11–12, 20–23, 24–36, 42–54, 59–60, 74, 76–77, 86–89, 100–103, 111, 116, 125

Feeling 8, 10, 21–22, 24, 46, 48, 73, 76, 93, 97, 111
Forgetting 20–21, 25, 31, 45, 112, 115, 118, 120

Genius 35, 48–49, 52–53, 57–60, 78
God 18, 27, 30, 69, 76–78, 92, 111
Gravity 7, 9, 66, 70–71, 74–75
Gravity and Grace 68–69
Grace 7, 9, 70–71, 74–75
Greene, Maxine 5–10, 86–89, 99–103

Hadot, Pierre 108
Happiness 5, 18, 21–22, 26–28, 39, 44–45, 47–48, 51–54, 112–113, 120
Happiness, Hope, and Despair 4–5
Hell 30, 44, 116–117
Hesse, Hermann 35
Hope 7–9, 11, 22–24, 26–27, 29, 31–32, 36, 73, 80, 89, 91–94, 111–113, 120, 125–126
Humility 7, 11, 56, 71, 74–75, 80, 89, 101, 125, 127

Illusions 22, 27
Immortality 10–11, 17, 92–93, 107–127
Impossibility 4, 80
Individual 4, 9, 17, 20, 31–32, 46, 57, 69, 71–74, 78–79, 98–100, 110–112, 120–121, 124–125
Intelligence 26, 57, 71–72

Kafka, Franz 10, 40, 86, 90, 95–96
Kierkegaard, Søren 30, 70, 85, 92, 110, 112, 124
Knowledge 1–2, 6, 20, 24–26, 33–34, 39–61, 69, 74, 80, 87, 89, 100–101, 115, 125–126
Knowing 41–48, 52–53, 57–60, 77, 80, 89, 125–126

Leopardi, Giacomo 5–8, 15–36
Levinas, Emmanuel 78
Light 5–6, 31, 46, 76
Limits 4, 12, 19, 26, 58, 69, 90, 92, 97, 110, 118, 126

Listening 7, 56, 71, 80, 100, 116
Longing 10, 29, 52, 110–113, 118, 123–124
Love 9, 18, 24, 35, 55, 72, 76–80, 92, 112–113, 117, 119–120, 123, 127
Lucretius 108

Madness 4, 10, 12, 86, 90–98, 103
Marx, Karl 69, 73
Memory 20–21, 50, 115, 118, 120
Montaigne, Michel de 124

Nature 2, 8, 17–24, 27, 31, 33–34, 42–43, 46–48, 54–55, 77, 101
Necessity 23, 42–43
Nietzsche, Friedrich 15, 30, 40, 70, 92, 94, 120
Numbers 4, 102

Obligations 9, 71–72, 75, 78, 99
Openness 3, 11, 56, 75, 79, 89, 100, 125, 127
Oppression and Liberty 68–69, 72, 74
Optimism 50, 53

Pain 19, 26–29, 31, 34, 43, 78, 116, 120, 127
Pessimism 7–8, 26
Plato 46, 51, 69, 72, 76, 108, 115
Possibilities 1, 7, 11–12, 52–54, 69, 74, 98–99, 103, 108, 110, 115, 117, 119, 124

Reason 8, 10, 17–24, 27, 30, 33, 41–43, 49, 52, 89–93, 102, 108, 110–112, 116
Religion 16, 18, 50, 68, 76, 92, 109, 111
Research 1, 39, 114–115
Rights 9, 71

Schopenhauer, Arthur 5–9, 15–16, 26, 35, 39–61, 92
Shadows 120
Socrates 10, 108
Spaces 4, 6, 9, 12, 60, 121
Stoics 10, 108
Stranger 10, 85–103, 117–118, 127
Striving 8, 40, 43–44, 58–60, 76, 112, 119
Struggle 27, 29, 31, 39, 46, 53, 58, 60, 73, 87, 93, 107, 111, 119
Sublime 12, 44–48, 52

Suffering 5–7, 9, 11, 19, 22, 26–31, 34–35, 41–45, 52–53, 58–61, 67, 71, 75, 78–79, 107, 112–113, 116, 118, 120–121
Surveillance 11, 122–123

Teacher as Stranger 10, 85–90
The Need for Roots 69, 71–72, 75
The Tragic Sense of Life 15, 28, 30, 110–113, 116
The World as Will and Representation 15, 40–61, 92
Truth 9, 19–20, 25, 31, 34, 56, 72, 74–76, 79, 92, 98, 103

Unamuno, Miguel de 5–7, 10, 15–16, 26, 28–31, 35, 43, 70, 92–94, 98, 103, 109–127

Uncertainty 3, 6–7, 11, 42, 81, 93, 100, 112, 117, 125–127
Unhappiness 2, 5, 8, 17–24, 27, 30–32, 35–36, 45, 48, 53–54
Unknowability 97, 103, 126

Waiting 7, 26, 71, 75, 77, 80, 116
Waiting for God 69, 78
Wants 9, 30, 45, 57–58, 98, 110, 112, 123
Weil, Simone 2, 5, 7–9, 11, 26, 32, 35, 45, 65–81, 98, 116, 122
Welcoming 89, 94, 99–100, 102
Will 8–9, 40–61
Will-less knowing 45–61
Wittgenstein, Ludwig 40, 70

Zibaldone di pensieri 8, 16–36

COMPLICATED CONVERSATION

A BOOK SERIES OF CURRICULUM STUDIES

Reframing the curricular challenge educators face after a decade of school deform, the books published in Peter Lang's Complicated Conversation Series testify to the ethical demands of our time, our place, our pro- fession. What does it mean for us to teach now, in an era structured by political polarization, economic destabi- lization, and the prospect of climate catastrophe? Each of the books in the Complicated Conversation Series provides provocative paths, theoretical and practical, to a very different future. In this resounding series of scholarly and pedagogical inter- ventions into the night- mare that is the present, we hear once again the sound of silence breaking, supporting us to rearticulate our pedagogical convictions in this time of terrorism, reframing curriculum as committed to the com- plicated conversation that is intercultural communication, self-understanding, and global justice.

The series editor is

> Dr. William F. Pinar
> Department of Curriculum Studies
> 2125 Main Mall
> Faculty of Education
> University of British Columbia
> Vancouver, British Columbia V6T 1Z4
> CANADA

To order other books in this series, please contact our Customer Service Department:

> peterlang@presswarehouse.com (within the U.S.)
> orders@peterlang.com (outside the U.S.)

Or browse online by series:

> www.peterlang.com

www.ingramcontent.com/pod-product-compliance
Lightning Source LLC
Chambersburg PA
CBHW052025290426
44112CB00014B/2384